20.-

COOPERATION

An Experimental Analysis

COOPERATION
An Experimental Analysis

Gerald Marwell
Department of Sociology
University of Wisconsin
Madison, Wisconsin

David R. Schmitt
Department of Sociology
University of Washington
Seattle, Washington

ACADEMIC PRESS   New York   San Francisco   London   **1975**

A Subsidiary of Harcourt Brace Jovanovich, Publishers

ACADEMIC PRESS, INC.
111 Fifth Avenue, New York, New York 10003

United Kingdom Edition published by
ACADEMIC PRESS, INC. (LONDON) LTD.
24/28 Oval Road, London NW1

Library of Congress Cataloging in Publication Data

Marwell, Gerald, Date
    Cooperation: an experimental analysis.

    Bibliography: p.
    Includes index.
    1.   Interpersonal relations.   I.   Schmitt, David R.,
joint author.   II.   Title.
HM132.M35   301.11   74-10204
ISBN 0−12−476350−2

PRINTED IN THE UNITED STATES OF AMERICA

To Bobbie and Fran
for helping to find a way out of
the Prisoner's Dilemma

CONTENTS

PREFACE

In most recent social psychology or sociology texts, cooperation is considered one of the "basic social processes." Indeed, a substantial amount of contemporary research either intentionally or unintentionally provides evidence concerning the factors related to such behavior. Yet no major book explicitly focusing on cooperation has appeared for more than 30 years (May & Doob, 1937).

This book represents our attempt to take a hard new look at cooperation, and contains the fruits of some 6 years of programmatic research on the topic. More than 30 interrelated experiments are reported in search of the factors that inhibit, maintain, or promote cooperation. Two of these factors are given particular attention—inequity and interpersonal risk between potential cooperators.

In contrast to the individualistic focus of most experimental research on cooperation, our approach has been molar. By molar we mean that we have treated *pairs* of individuals (groups), not the individuals themselves, as our units of analysis. This procedure stems both from our bias as sociologists and from seminal work on cooperation by N. Azrin, O. Lindsley, and D. Cohen. Their work toward the development of an unambiguously defined, readily repeatable, cooperative response suggested to us the feasibility of a programmatic investigation of variables that promote cooperation.

By taking a molar approach we were able to apply some of the key methodological and theoretical insights of behavioral analysis to a group response. Drawing on Cohen's (1962) and Lindsley's (1966) research with children, we first developed a simple response which reflects the main conceptual characteristics of cooperation. We were then able to investigate experimentally the extent to which this behavioral response could be controlled by relevant environmental contingencies. At the methodological level these experiments constitute the first systematic application of intrapair replication procedures (ABA design) to moderate-sized samples of human groups. By studying each group for a number of hours, involving thousands of responses, we were able to demonstrate the clear and precise experimental control that can be exercised over cooperative behavior.

The level of control we obtained was also a function of the particular alternative to cooperation that we provided to our subjects. Unlike the setting in most traditional research on cooperation, the major alternative for our subjects was neither competition nor doing nothing. Instead, subjects could choose to work individually—probably the most common "real-world" alternative to cooperative behavior. Interestingly, however, the question of competition reentered the research at a later stage. Reformulated as interpersonal risk—the potential for an aversive response by either partner—it emerged as one of the key *independent* variables for analysis. When group members were later given the opportunity to take money that the other had earned through collective effort, the rate of cooperation was dramatically reduced. Not because group members engaged in continuous competition, but because they retreated to self-protective individual work. The central problem of trust and protectiveness for the maintenance of cooperation thus became apparent. In everyday life, however, cooperation does emerge, despite the ubiquity of risk. Thus, we began the systematic pursuit of those factors which reduce the impact of risk, and promote cooperation. Our findings both underscored the fragility of cooperative behavior and suggested some minimal social conditions under which cooperation will persist.

ACKNOWLEDGMENTS

The cooperative, collective nature of this work is strikingly illustrated by reporting our debts to many colleagues and aides, although we accept for ourselves alone any deserved blame.

First, however, a heartfelt thanks to our sponsor. The National Science Foundation provided the bulk of support for this research with three substantial grants (GS-843, GS-1695, and GS-28087). At key points in the development of the research program The University of Wisconsin Research Committee also provided support. The University of Oslo and the Norwegian Peace Research Institute provided space for our Norwegian venture.

Three people deserve special mention. Dr. Robert Shotola collaborated with us at the early stages of the program, and co-authored the most extensive paper incorporated in this book. He also provided suggestions and encouragement at subsequent stages. Bjørn Bøyesen translated our experimental materials into Norwegian, ran all Norwegian subjects, translated their behavior into English, and collaborated in the analysis and writing of the article based on these data. Sandra Adkisson Tausend was an equal in the development and execution of the study with children relating cooperative behavior to inequity reported at the end of Chapter 3.

Six people put in extended tours of duty with the program, and assumed major responsibilities for its progress: James Besser, Susan Brandscheid, Ira Kaufman, Cheryl Keeton, Connie Tesch Kolpin, and Richard Shurman.

The list of experimenters, stooges, and schedulers who have worked in the program includes many who gave us more than just their time, but took a serious intellectual interest in the project: Ruth Ames, Sharon Bartman, Vicki Burton, Peggy Bushnell, Janet Chorlton, Jeanne Condon, Sara Connor, Sharon Cornell, Catherine Cummins, Martha Dilts, Kathleen Ehrenberg, Charlotte Farr, Jane Hauser, Fran Hawkins, Rita Hurbi, Karen Lee, Nancy Light, Marilyn Muehrer, Marilyn Ratliff, Marya Roland, Robin Ross, Mary Ann Rundell, Lane Simpson, Joyce Solochek, Dennis Statz, Carol Stolte, David Tucker, and Sue Wolfe.

The task of typing and assembling the various manuscript drafts was handled expertly by Beulah Reddaway and her staff at the University of Washington. The index was primarily the work of Deborah McDonald. From a long list of colleagues and friends, the following deserve particular mention: Robert Burgess, Herbert L. Costner, Weldon Johnson, H. Andrew Michener, L. Keith Miller, and Shalom Schwartz.

CREDITS

Some of the materials in this book were presented in articles we have published in professional journals. The following list contains the complete reference for each of these previous papers, in temporal order. We thank the various journals for their permission to reproduce these materials:

Figure A-1, p. 192. Schmitt, David R. & Marwell, Gerald. Stimulus control in the experimental study of cooperation. *Journal of the Experimental Analysis of Behavior,* 1968, 11, 571-574. Copyright 1968 by the Society for the Experimental Analysis of Behavior, Inc.

COOPERATION

An Experimental Analysis

CHAPTER 1

INTRODUCTION: THE STUDY OF COOPERATION

Some think cooperation is *the* question: "It is not the atomic bomb that will destroy civilization. But civilized society can destroy itself—finally, no doubt; with bombs—if it fails to understand intelligently and to control the aids and deterrents to cooperation [Mayo, 1945, p. xvi]." Unfortunately, this is not a book about saving the world, nor a book about war, except as the reader would have it so. This is a book about people getting together to accomplish some specifiable task—and about others trying to carry out the task alone—in laboratories, under highly controlled, highly "artificial" conditions. It is a record of our search, through more than 30 experiments, for some of the reasons that individuals do not cooperate more.

Our negative phrasing of the problem—why *don't* people cooperate more—is not accidental. It is our conviction that although examples of interpersonal cooperation may be easily found, individualism in goal achievement is much more common in this, and in probably every other society. However, a very large number of tasks that people do alone would be more efficiently completed by some joint effort. Efficiency through specialization and the division of labor is a common principle. Capitalization through the pooling of resources is a necessity for many projects and purchases. Why don't more of us belong to buying cooperatives, or home maintenance cooperatives, or infant care groups? Why don't more people join in business partnerships of various kinds? Though the communal living movement has had its theoreticians for a very long time, and its adherents for even longer, communes have always found it very hard to survive. Why? Why is it so hard to organize political action groups, and to keep them going once they are organized?

These are more than just practical problems. In the writings of many major theorists, the question of why cooperation does or does not occur occupies a prominent place. According to Robert Nisbet:

> In one form or another speculative or reflective interest in cooperation is as old as human thought . . . . From Confucius, Lao-tzu, and Guatame in the Far East as from the prophets of the Old Testament, the centrality of the ethic and psychology of cooperation may be easily inferred. For both Plato and Aristotle, cooperation was the keystone of the good state [Nisbet, 1968, p. 386].

Each of the major social sciences has accorded the problem of cooperation considerable interest. Irving Louis

Horowitz has gone so far as to call cooperation the central problem in sociological theory:

> This history of conflict and consensus (theories) has been a dialogue between exclusive frames of reference seeking to explain the same phenomenon—human cooperation [Horowitz, 1968, p. 6].

Undoubtedly the most vigorous continuing attack on the question of cooperation, however, has been in social psychology. An early landmark in this stream of research was the publication of *Competition and Cooperation* (1937) by May and Doob, which contained a comprehensive review of the relevant psychological, sociological, anthropological, and life history literature. A series of general propositions was presented, focusing on conditions which affect the occurrence, character, and effectiveness of cooperative or competitive relations. The focus of the book is perhaps best understood in terms of the dominant social phenomenon and intellectual question of the time: the Great Depression and the relative merits of capitalist and socialist forms of economic organization.

If the Great Depression concentrated attention on such organizational issues, World War II might be considered the impetus for a subsequent shift in focus. In the work of Deutsch, Krauss, and Rapoport, among others, the central question became the emergence of conflict. If two (or more) persons are given cooperation or competition as alternative modes of response, what are the factors which lead them to the one rather than the other? The currently prevalent form of this research resulted from the introduction of game theory as a conceptual tool. The Prisoner's Dilemma and its variations still constitute the dominant paradigm for research on conflict, although new perspectives are currently emerging (see, for example, Swingle, 1970).

Our own approach follows primarily from this social-psychological tradition. However, our focal concern is cooperation, not conflict—and the factors that encourage, inhibit, sustain, or destroy this form of behavior. Our approach is experimental: it investigates cooperation in the minimal unit of interest—dyads—and concentrates on specifying the situational conditions that affect the probability of a pair of persons performing a cooperative task. A prior concern, however, and the one which occupies the next part of this chapter, is a more detailed consideration of the concept itself. Exactly what is it we mean when we talk about "cooperation"? How much consensus on the meaning of the term is there in the literature? What variant of cooperation should we select for our operational definition?

THE CONCEPT OF COOPERATION

Consider the variety of "real-world" examples of cooperation: a team of surgeons performing a delicate operation; a football team scoring a touchdown; two scholars collaborating in writing a book; a political party electing its candidate; factory workers assembling automobiles; two children lifting a third to pull apples off a tree. To the casual observer, whatever commonalities these examples have may seem to be buried by their differences. The closely synchronized, carefully planned, intimate job of the surgeons is not much like the raucous, loose, helter-skelter election campaign. The hundreds of assembly-line workers whose activities are meshed by clocks, signal lights, and foremen work differently from two authors, each writing alone, each bringing his work to the other for criticism and suggestion, and ordered by no third party.

Such diversity is reflected in the equally varied formal

definitions of cooperation posed by social scientists. Consider the following representative examples:

MAY AND DOOB (1937): "Behavior directed toward the same social end by at least two individuals . . . (the end) can be achieved by all or almost all of the individuals concerned [p. 6]."

DEUTSCH (1949a): A situation in which "a goal region can be entered (to some degree) by any given individual . . . only if all the individuals . . . can also enter their respective goal regions (to some degree) [p. 132]."

KELLER AND SCHOENFELD (1950): A situation in which "the combined behavior of two or more organisms is needed to procure positive, or remove negative reinforcement for either . . . . Cooperation involves two things: (1) each organism's action must be discriminative for the other's performance; and (2) each organism must be reinforced for the part it plays in the cooperative scheme [pp. 357–8]."

PARSONS (1951): "The meshing of activities or 'contributions' in such a way that the outcome is a unit which as a unit can enter into the exchange process [p. 72]."

HOMANS (1961): Cooperation occurs when, by emitting activities to one another, or by emitting activities in concert to the environment, at least two men achieve a greater total reward than either could have achieved by working alone [p. 384]."

NISBET (1968): "Cooperation is a joint or collaborative behavior that is directed toward some goal in which there is common interest or hope of reward [p. 384]."

As exemplified in these definitions, most observers do not conceive of cooperation as a simple behavior, nor even as a specific pattern of behaviors. Rather, it is seen as a set of relations among behaviors and their consequences. Viewing such past conceptualizations collectively, we may distill five specific elements which define the content of cooperative relations: goal-directed behavior, rewards for each participant, distributed responses, coordination, and social coordination. Various definitions may be seen as focusing on particular elements from this set.

Of the five basic elements, two—*goal-directed behavior* and *rewards for each participant*-have been viewed as central by almost all writers, although the language which has described these elements has often been quite different. Thus, May and Doob refer to behavior directed toward "social ends"; Deutsch refers to entry into "goal regions"; Parsons describes the "meshing of activities" leading to "outcomes which as a unit can enter the exchange process."

Kelley and Thibaut (1968) use the terms conjunctive or disjunctive to denote the presence or absence of *distributed responses*—the third element. When the task requirement is conjunctive, success depends on all persons making the correct response; there is a division of labor. For example, assembly-line production requires that each of a number of workers assemble one of the specified parts. When the task requirement is disjunctive, the correct response is needed from only one or some of the participants. A group attempting to solve a mathematical problem needs to have only one person discover the answer.

When the task requires a division of labor, the possibility of the fourth element, *coordination,* arises. Must the cooperative behaviors take place in some specified relation? For example, a team of surgeons must precisely coordinate their activities to be successful. Investors pooling their resources need not.

Coordination is rarely successful without the use of cues to synchronize activites. In many situations these cues are mechanical. The effectiveness of most large groups—factories, bureaucracies—or small groups in which the members are not in face-to-face contact, rests on the use of clocks, memos, intercoms, and the like. Lewis Mumford (1934) has suggested that the industrial revolution rested more on the invention of the clock than on the commonly noted steam engine. In other situations, the coordinating cues may be social, where one person is actually monitoring the behavior of another. The requirement of *social coordination* is the fifth element.

Although not traditionally part of the definition, a description of cooperation would not be complete without some reference to time. One aspect is the length of time during which the onset of all responses must occur—the latency of the cooperative response (Volger, 1969). Another is the length of time required for each of the component responses.

These five elements of cooperation may be combined in various ways to define several "types" of cooperation. In particular, several of the elements form a logical chain in which each successive element assumes the presence of the previous elements. Thus, social coordination requires coordination per se, and both assume that responses are distributed. These linkages simplify the typology presented in Table 1-1. It is assumed that rewards for each participant and goal-directed behavior are required elements in all definitions of cooperation, and the typology is constructed on this basis. Listed on the right-hand side of the table are some of the writers who have used the specified definition.

SELECTING A CONCEPTUAL DEFINITION

As is perhaps typical of any close analysis of a common concept, the above discussion provides no basis for selecting a single "best" definition of cooperation. Instead, it points to the diverse phenomena which could be considered instances of cooperation, depending upon the selection of elements. For example, with the inclusion of all five elements, instances of cooperation would be limited to very small groups, such as athletic teams or construction crews,

Table 1-1

Types of Cooperation

Definitions	Goal-directed behavior	Rewards for each participant	Distributed responses	Coordination	Social coordination	Conceptual definitions
I	×	×				Maller (1929), Deutsch (1949), Zajonc (1966), Smead (1972)
II	×	×	×			Weingarten and Mechner (1966), May and Doob (1937)
III	×	×	×	×		Parsons (1951), Homans (1961), Lundberg, Schrag, and Larsen (1963), Nisbet (1968)
IV	×	×	×	×	×	Keller and Schoenfeld (1950)

Elements

in which the participants monitor one another's activities. As elements are deleted from the definition the range of cases subsumed grows progressively larger. For example, if the requirement of social coordination is removed, cooperation could include various bureaucratic settings or manufacturing processes where the coordinating cues are impersonal. With little or no coordination required, cooperation could also include a wide variety of scientific and industrial settings where the cumulative contributions of various persons over time culminate in an invention or discovery. Without distributed responses, cooperation would also include the many cases where some of the persons who are rewarded have engaged in few or none of the activities producing them—for example, the benefits from a discovery, or the negotiation of a treaty.

Not only does the choice of elements determine the type of situation defined as cooperative, it is also likely to specify the effects of other variables on cooperation. For example, in the simplest case, where task responses are not distributed, only some persons need have the required problem-solving skills in order for the response to be made. However, if task responses are distributed, another consideration emerges: the degree to which persons with the necessary skills are matched with the required tasks. If response coordination is also required, adequate information distribution and task planning become critical. Finally, if face-to-face contact is also required, the importance of various personal characteristics such as demeanor, age, and sex may come into play in determining the ease with which the participants interact. Systematic studies have yet to be undertaken to show that these factors do indeed operate to prevent the generalization of findings across the several types of cooperative settings. However, with such important differences, generalization may be highly problematic.

Which still leaves the question of which definition of

cooperation our own procedures should reflect. In the absence of compelling arguments for the selection of any one definition, the choice becomes somewhat arbitrary. We have decided to use the most restrictive definition, which contains all five elements noted above. This alternative has two major benefits. First, the generalization of any findings to other settings is facilitated by the full specification of conditions. Findings from a setting with fewer elements may be contingent on some value of the unspecified elements. If these unspecified conditions are not duplicated in other conditions, generality will not be achieved. Secondly, comparison of our findings with previous empirical research would appear to be clearer with a restrictive definition, since any restrictive component of a previous setting would be contained as well in ours.

CHARACTERISTICS OF THE ANALYSIS

With a definition of cooperation, however arbitrary, in hand, our next step was the selection of major independent variables. This process was importantly affected by two general characteristics which distinguish this research from many of the previous studies—its scope and level of analysis.

Scope. A review of the literature on cooperation reveals a diverse array of experimental settings with a variety of defining characteristics. However, most of these settings were designed to study the effects of some specific variable on cooperation. Thus, not surprisingly, little is known about the comparative or combined effects of such variables, given the problematic nature of comparison across settings. In the research presented here, two settings with similar defining characteristics will be used to investigate the effects of a variety of variables, both singly and in combination. Some of these variables have emerged as relevant in other cooperative settings with quite different character-istics. Others have not been studied experimentally in a cooperative context.

Within the limits of the laboratory both the short- and long-term effects of various conditions will also be investi-gated. Usual experimental procedures involve the study of no more than several hundred cooperative acts over a several-hour period. It may be, however, that behavior pat-terns resulting in such a short time span are transitory. Thus, procedures in many of the present experiments will include multiple sessions and thousands of task responses.

Level of Analysis. Two approaches have contributed variables relevant to the problem of cooperation. One, a psychological approach, focuses on individual characteris-tics of the participants. These include personality charac-teristics as well as more situationally specific perceptions of the task and participants. The other, a situational approach, focuses on variables which define the setting, including task characteristics, reward conditions, and modes of inter-action. Over the past decade a large literature has accumu-lated within each tradition with particular emphasis on prediction within mixed motive games, most notably the Prisoner's Dilemma. In general, subjective variables have not been strongly predictive of cooperative behavior (Druckman, 1971). A major problem concerning the use of subjective variables is that of measurement. As hypothe-tical constructs, subjective variables require some kind of observable behavior as an index, and to date there is no inventory of subjective variables with established validity and reliability to predict cooperative behavior. In addition, subjective variables are difficult to manipulate experi-mentally, usually requiring severe assumptions concerning the relation between the operations actually engaged in by the experimenter and the construct of interest. By contrast, a number of studies report stronger effects for a variety of situational variables, either alone or in interaction with other situational or psychological variables (for a review see Druckman, 1971). More important, situational variables typically can be measured with a high degree of reliability, and are more likely to be manipulated easily and unambiguously in both experimental and nonexperimental settings.

For these reasons, our concern first will be with identifying situational variables that affect cooperation. Our primary focus will be on cooperation as a molar entity which, as we have defined it, includes the joint activity of more than one person. Subsequently we will consider the cooperativeness of individuals, which may or may not result in cooperation.

MAJOR INDEPENDENT VARIABLES: INEQUITY AND INTERPERSONAL RISK

Before discussing the variables of major concern, we should note a category of variables which, for the sake of manageability, we will not be considering in depth. These are variables which concern the ability of persons to perform the cooperative response itself. Factors such as task complexity, response feedback, and stimuli that indicate the presence of potential cooperators are among those which make the cooperative response problematic. While of obvious importance (see, for example, Roby, 1968), many of these variables are also closely tied to the particular cooperative task employed and therefore are of less general concern. We will thus begin by assuming that potential cooperators are able to cooperate.

Inequity. In considering variables likely to be salient in cooperative groups, we began with the basic relationship between behavior and rewards. With single subjects, two primary aspects of rewards may be varied: their magnitude, for example, large or small; and the schedule on which they are delivered, for example, frequently or infrequently, regularly or intermittently. Rewards of sufficient size and frequency are, of course, requisite for the maintenance of most behaviors, including cooperation, and thus are not treated as problematic here. What is of concern is a third aspect of rewards—one which emerges only when more than one person is rewarded at a time—their comparative magnitude.

This variable, which necessarily characterizes relationships entailing mutual rewards, is clearly important to the study of cooperation. Within cooperating groups, members are most commonly aware not only of each other, but of what rewards each is receiving. Thus, each person will probably compare his own rewards with those of his partners, and use them as standards in determining satisfaction with the relationship.

In the literature concerning the interpersonal comparison of rewards, the key question has been whether the rewards are considered "equitable" or "fair." A major social-psychological theory—"equity theory"—has developed around this theme. Research based on this theory has concerned the effects of inequity on emotions, cognitions, and behavior (Walster *et al.*, 1973).

Although inequity as conceptualized here is clearly a property of groups, most prior consideration of its effects focuses on individual response. The classic statement concerning the alternatives available to individuals who are being rewarded inequitably is that of Adams (1965). Included are four basic behavioral responses (Adams also suggests two subjective responses with which we are not here concerned). The individual may:

1. Alter his inputs (that is, work, investments) into

the cooperative activity. Unequal rewards may be judged "equitable" if the inputs of the group members are proportionate to their share of the rewards. Thus, the subject who feels underpaid might reduce the quantity or quality of his work as a means of producing equity.

2. Alter the reward distribution so that it is less inequitable. This response requires that the actor have some control over the initial reward distribution or that he be able to transfer rewards to other actors after they have been distributed.

3. Withdraw from the activity. This is a particularly important alternative for cooperative groups, which rely on the contribution of all members and for whom the withdrawal of a single member may make cooperation among the remaining members impossible.

4. Try to entice another member to withdraw from the group. This too is potentially disruptive, for the same reasons as for withdrawal.

Most previous research on the effects of inequity has focused on the first of these four responses. In considering effects on cooperation, however, the two most relevant behavioral responses appear to be withdrawal and the redistribution of rewards. Cooperative tasks for very small groups, including the one used in this research, frequently require a high degree of coordination and mutual dependency, and permit little or no latitude in the types of coordinated activities required for reward. Each person must perform that part of the task assigned to him. Any changes from prespecified performances are really equivalent to nonperformance in that the requirements for reinforcement are not met. Thus, changing one's work (input) may have the same consequences as withdrawal from cooperation. On the other hand, the potential for reward redistribution is common in small cooperative groups. Although individual members may be differentially rewarded by external sources, the rewards can often be transferred, provided the appropriate mechanisms are available within the group.

Interpersonal Risk. The second major variable to be considered—interpersonal risk—is another element particularly salient in cooperative groups. Consider the realities of cooperation. More often than not, an individual who enters a cooperative relationship substantially reduces the extent of his personal control over the consequences he may experience. By accepting dependency on another person, he also incurs the element of risk. This added risk may arise in several ways. If the task to be performed requires a division of labor, a person's own efforts, however strenuous or expert, may go unrewarded if his partner does not adequately perform his share of the work. A tennis partner may play poorly. A coauthor may be unable to write his part of the book. A trapeze catcher may forget to dry his hands!

A different type of risk occurs when cooperation entails joint access to and control of resources. Research teams share relevant technologies. Business partners pool capital. Families share material possessions. In these cases, each person runs the risk that his resources may be taken or destroyed by the other. Trade secrets are sold or stolen. Company funds are misused or embezzled. Family breakups are settled inequitably. Unlike performance failure, which implies mutual loss, this second type of interpersonal risk may involve substantial gain for one party. It is with the effects of this second form of risk—the risk of reward loss through expropriation—that we are concerned.

On the individual level, the impact of interpersonal risk relates to the problem of trust. This problem has been central to Deutsch's (1962) extensive individual-level analysis of cooperation. As defined by Deutsch, a situation with a choice to trust or not trust is one in which another person has the potential to administer both harmful and beneficial consequences, but where the potential for the former outweighs the latter. If a person chooses to place himself in such a situation, he is making a trusting choice. The problem of trust underlies the dilemma in the widely studied Prisoner's Dilemma, and this is the form of research used by Deutsch and many subsequent investigators. In Chapter 4 we discuss some of the limitations of this approach.

The problem of trust is often solved in everyday life. People do cooperate, despite risk. Thus, the next logical question is why? What are the factors which produce trust despite interpersonal risk? Our research on this problem focuses on several paths toward the establishment of cooperation under risk. Each is comparable to a form of social control over interaction that is common in everyday life. One path emphasizes the establishment of protective conditions which make violations of trust difficult or nonprofitable. The second involves forming a personal association between potential cooperators, within which violations of trust would threaten the maintenance of the relationship. The third focuses on the salience of broader societal norms, which define violation of interpersonal trust as unacceptable. The last focuses on a response through which a single person may promote cooperation—"pacifism."

PLAN OF THE BOOK

Although the basic structure of our approach to causes of cooperation has not changed substantially over time, the above represents the distillation of our thinking after an opportunity to reflect on the research reported below. Thus, the presentation of materials will not coincide completely with the order in which variables are discussed above. Instead, we shall pay some (although not complete) attention to the actual historical sequence of the studies we undertook.

We therefore begin in Chapter 2 by describing the development of our operational definition of cooperation. Chapter 3 then contains the first set of experiments, which describe the effects of inequity. Chapter 4 reports the basic experiments on the effects of interpersonal risk, while Chapter 5 presents a series of experiments testing the generality of that effect. Chapters 6, 7, and 8 report experiments attempting to introduce factors which could mitigate the risk effect. The final chapter presents the summary and conclusions.

CHAPTER 2

METHODS: MEASUREMENT AND EXPERIMENTAL DESIGN

The number of conceptual definitions of cooperation has been paralleled by the development of a wide array of research settings, each involving a particular kind of cooperative response. The features of these settings have been dictated in great part by the kinds of problems they were designed to study. After reviewing this literature, we selected one of these settings as the basis for the present research. Analysis of its characteristics, however, led to

19

the need for modification. This chapter contains a description of the setting which evolved and the reasons for its selection. We then present the experimental procedures generally used throughout the research.

Previous Settings

A review of the literature reveals that few of the settings which have been used for the experimental study of cooperation include all of the criterion elements detailed in Chapter 1. In general, two types of settings have been used: those which focus on the *choice* to cooperate; and those concerned with the factors that determine the *effectiveness* with which persons cooperate. Of the settings focusing on cooperative choice, the most widely studied have been simple "mixed-motive" matrix games, particularly the Prisoner's Dilemma. Responses made by subjects in these games are minimal, consisting only of opting for either the cooperative or competitive outcome, and involve no coordination or division of labor.

Studies of factors determining the effectiveness of cooperation have tended to use complex tasks in order to make a correct response problematic. Examples[1] include tasks which require highly coordinated individual responses (e.g., Wegner & Zeaman, 1956; Azrin & Lindsley, Ghiselli & Lodahl, 1958; Smelser, 1961; Egerman, 1966; Mithaug & Burgess, 1968); tasks in which participants receive ambiguous response feedback (e.g. Sidowski, Wyckoff, & Tabory, 1956; Rosenberg & Hall, 1958); tasks in which participants must bargain (e.g. Deutsch & Krauss, 1962); or tasks which require that information dispersed

[1]See Hake and Vukelich (1972) for a useful typology of what they term "performance" tasks.

over several persons be pooled, as in widely studied "discussion groups" or "communication networks" (e.g., Deutsch, 1949b; Leavitt, 1958).

THE PROGENITOR: COHEN AND LINDSLEY'S SETTING

The setting that provided the basis for the present research was developed by Cohen (1962) and Lindsley (1966) and requires a coordinated response. Using the same basic apparatus but with varying sets of contingencies, Cohen and Lindsley conducted a series of experiments to investigate rates of cooperation or competition under various social conditions. In the variation of concern here, subjects could make either a rewarded cooperative response or an unrewarded nonsocial one.

Briefly, two subjects, seated in separate laboratory rooms, each faced a panel containing a plunger, stimulus lights, and a dispenser for pennies and candy. Both subjects were rewarded for a cooperative response whenever one pulled his plunger within .5 second of the other. Each cooperative response was followed by a 2.5-second time-out in which the room was darkened and a loud tone sounded. In the variation of the setting most relevant here, a subject's pull was indicated to his teammate by the illumination of a light on the latter's panel (henceforth, the "response light").

This setting was of particular interest for several reasons. First, it appeared to include all five elements of cooperation. Second, unlike most other tasks, it was a simple free-operant response which could be both readily learned and rapidly performed. The free-operant characteristic meant that the task could be repeated at any time (after the time-out), thus permitting the study of variations in response rate as well as the presence or absence of cooperation. A task that may be rapidly performed also permits the observation of a large amount of activity within a short period of time.

For our investigation, however, the Cohen–Lindsley apparatus had two major drawbacks. First, under certain circumstances cooperation could be achieved without either subject attending to the other's behavior. Second, there were no independent, rewarding alternatives to cooperation.

MODIFYING THE COHEN–LINDSLEY SETTING

Social Coordination. The Cohen–Lindsley setting was designed to require that in making a cooperative response there would be social interaction, that is, the subject pulling his plunger second would be reacting to the behavior of his partner. Lindsley (1966) suggests that the .5 second within which the subjects' responses must be coordinated is sufficiently short to avoid cooperation merely by chance. A closer inspection of the setting, however, suggests that subjects may achieve cooperative responses without attention to their partners. For example, if both subjects simply respond at very high rates (in excess of 120 plunger pulls per minute), some response pairs will necessarily "coordinate." Similarly, if both subjects respond immediately after a timeout, a cooperative response results. If these occur frequently, the behavior of the subjects may not be interpreted with confidence as being "social," that is, at least one of the two individuals is responding to the behavior of the other. Consequently, the Cohen–Lindsley task was modified to assure that cooperative responses were based on social cues.

The key element in this modification was the introduction of a delay between the responses of the two subjects as a requirement for cooperation. Either subject could pull his plunger first. His pull illuminated his partner's response light for 3 seconds. Both subjects were rewarded if the second subject pulled his plunger within .5 second after the response light went off. To make the maximum response rate on the modified task comparable to that on the original task, the timeout following reward was reduced from 5 to 2 seconds. Thus, with the 3-second interval between rewarded responses, a minimum of 5 seconds had to elapse between rewarded responses. Figure 2-1 illustrates cooperative response requirements for the modified task with Subject A responding first. Subject B can respond first as well.

MODIFIED TASK

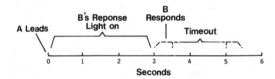

Figure 2-1 *Response requirements for the modified task (Person A responding first).*

To demonstrate that modification of the Cohen–Lindsley task assures social coordination, we conducted an experiment which is reported in full in Appendix A. The experiment examined subjects in both the modified and original Cohen–Lindsley settings under conditions where social stimuli for cooperation were either present or absent. Conditions in which social stimuli were absent were created by disconnecting the response light (the light on the subject's panel which flashed whenever his partner made a plunger pull). With this light inoperative, a subject did not know when his partner made a response. Hence, there could be no coordination by attending to the other's behavior. Results of the experiment clearly demonstrated that high rates of cooperation could be maintained in the original setting even with the response lights off. In the modified setting, however, very few cooperative responses were achieved when social cues for coordination were absent.

Task Choice. In constructing a setting in which the conditions affecting the choice to cooperate could be investigated, the availability of an easily learned, rapidly performed cooperative task was the first requisite. However, some evidence suggests that limiting the setting to a single task alternative is probably not most conducive to studying (or even interpreting) the effects of conditions which inhibit or facilitate choice. It is also desirable to provide subjects with some rewarding alternative response. For most subjects, a laboratory is probably never a neutral stimulus—they at least presume that the experimenter is concerned with some aspect of their behavior, not their absence of behavior. Thus, subjects are likely to be active rather than inactive, regardless of the experimental consequences (Webb, Campbell, Schwartz, & Sechrest, 1966; Wiggins, 1968). Experimental studies with nonhuman subjects have found that a single reinforced response is more difficult to eliminate than one with one or more reinforcing alternatives available (concurrent operants). For example, an intensity of punishment which has little effect on the response rate of a single operant can almost completely suppress the response when an alternative, although less reinforcing, is present (Azrin & Holz, 1966). It should also be noted that outside the laboratory a choice among at least several activities is typically available. Thus, it was on more than just empirical grounds that we decided to include an alternative task to cooperation in our research setting, and to provide the subjects with task choice procedures.

As a research question, task choice has perhaps the longest history in the literature on cooperation. But almost always the same two alternatives have been offered—cooperation or competition. From early research on problem-solving groups to current studies using the Prisoner's

Dilemma and other "mixed-motive" games, the alternative to cooperation has been conflict. Certainly this opposition is not fundamental, either practically or in the theoretical literature. A more common alternative to cooperation in most situations is probably individual effort—working alone. For most persons, the market for their efforts is larger than the amount they produce. Thus, the scarcity of rewards which leads to competition is relatively infrequent. As Margaret Mead noted in her cross-cultural research on cooperation,

> We found it necessary to emphasize that the terms cooperative and competitive were not opposite, as they are so loosely used in popular speech. To make our analysis complete we had to have a third category which we called *individualistic* behavior, that is, behavior in which the individual strives toward his goal without reference to others [Mead, 1937, p. 16].

Thus, an individual alternative to cooperation was provided in our research. Subjects could work by themselves on an individual task at a rate similar to that for cooperation. By working alone the subject could withdraw from all interaction with his partner and still earn money. Inactivity on either task was still possible as well.

The subjects themselves controlled which of the tasks, cooperative or individual, could be performed. By flicking a switch each subject selected either the individual or cooperative task. In order for the cooperative task to be operative, both subjects had to choose to work together. One could not work cooperatively while the other worked alone. If either subject chose to work alone, the other subject also had to work alone.

Setting Characteristics and Procedures

All experiments used a setting defined by the cooperative and individual alternatives. In addition, these experiments employed procedures which followed a common logic. In each experiment a comprehensive training sequence was followed by a procedure in which the behavior of each pair was studied both in the presence and in the absence of a condition potentially disruptive of cooperation. At this point, we will describe in detail the first setting, and present an overview of the general experimental procedures.

THE STANDARD SETTING

The experiments were conducted in a laboratory consisting of two separate subject rooms and an adjacent experimenter's room containing the control and recording apparatus. A sketch of the subject room is shown in Fig. 2-2. Each of the rooms contained a table-mounted panel 9 by 18 inches (23 by 46 cm). Background (white) noise in each room was used to block any sounds from the experimenter's room or an adjacent hallway. The panel in each room contained a plunger (Lindsley knob), a switch for choosing to

Figure 2-2 *Diagram of standard experimental setting.*

work on the cooperative or individual task, stimulus lights, and two add–subtract counters (see Fig. 2-3 for a schematic presentation). All functions were labeled. The red light in the upper corner of the panel indicated when the tasks were operative. The white light in the lower corner illuminated for .1 or 3 seconds whenever the other subject made a response. The blue light indicated when the other subject moved his switch to cooperate. The green lights next to the counters flashed for every reinforcement count registered. Each count was worth .1 ¢. One counter showed the subject his own earnings during the current 2-hour session, while the other showed his partner's earnings. For all sessions after the first, both subjects' previous totals were posted on a blackboard on the wall directly behind the panel. A closed circuit television receiver placed next to the panel showed the amount of money available to each subject for work on each of the tasks.

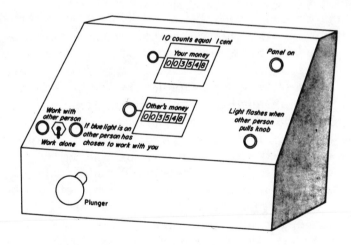

Figure 2-3 *Diagram of subject panel.*

SUBJECTS

The procedures used to recruit subjects varied somewhat from those most common in the discipline. In particular, we wanted to ensure that money, the primary reinforcer throughout the experiment, would motivate our subjects to work to maximize earnings. Consequently, our recruitment procedures were designed to dissuade from volunteering those persons primarily interested in obtaining an "educational" experience. Such subjects might be comparatively insensitive to monetary consequences. With the exception of one sample of grade school children, subjects in the first experiments were college students at either the University of Wisconsin or the University of Washington who responded to a bulletin posted in the student employment office or read in undergraduate classes. It asked for volunteers "who would like to earn some money," and stressed that participation was "not of any special educational value since it only involves work on a simple laboratory task." Subjects were scheduled for experimental sessions on the basis of mutual availability and lack of acquaintance. Since any contact between subjects outside the experiment could introduce uncontrolled and unknown motivating effects, for example, friendship or agreements on how to respond, persons from the same address were never scheduled together, and subjects were prevented from meeting one another during the experiment. Prior to each session subjects reported to separate waiting rooms in the laboratory area and were escorted individually to their experimental rooms. Likewise, at the end of each session they were dismissed from the laboratory area several minutes apart. Subjects worked no more than one session per day. Typically, consecutive sessions were separated by no more than two or three days.

Table 2-1

Conditions Defining Training Session

Segment	Counts[a]		Length of segment
	Cooperation	Individual	
1. Cooperation only	6	none	335 cooperative responses
2. Cooperation or indi-vidual responding	1	6	135 individual responses
3. Cooperation or indi-vidual responding	6	1	135 cooperative responses
4. Baseline: cooperation or individual res-ponding	3[b]	2[b]	15 minutes

[a]Each count was worth .1¢.
[b]Four for cooperation and three for individual responding in later experiments.

TRAINING PROCEDURE

To assure task comprehension, all college student subjects participated in a 1.5–2-hour training session during which they demonstrated their ability to perform the two tasks in response to differences in earnings. The various segments of this session are summarized in Table 2-1.

Subjects were instructed first in the operation of the cooperative task. The experimenter read instructions over an intercom which led subjects through the steps required to make a cooperative response. To begin this response either subject could pull his plunger first, thus illuminating the white response light on the other's panel for 3 seconds. Reinforcement (a counter advance of six points for each subject) occurred whenever the second subject pulled his plunger in the .5-second period after the response light went out. This response illuminated the response light on the first subject's panel for .1 second. If the second subject pulled the knob before, or more than .5 second after the response light went off, no counter advance occurred. Then the next pull by either subject reinitiated the other's response light for 3 seconds. If the subject responding first pulled more than once without a pull by the other subject, his additional pulls reinitiated the other's response light for 3 seconds. Each reward was followed by a 2-second period during which cooperative responses were not rewarded. The red panel light was turned off during this period. Following the instructions, subjects worked until 335 cooperative responses had been made.

Next, the individual task and the use of the task selection switch were demonstrated. On the individual task each pull of the plunger advanced the counter and illuminated the response light on the other subject's panel for .1 second. In order to equate the maximum frequency of reward under the individual and cooperative task conditions, each individual response was followed by a 5-second period in which the red panel light was turned off and responses were not rewarded.

Each subject could choose to work on either the individual or cooperative task by operating the toggle switch on his panel. The cooperative task could be performed only if both subjects chose to work together. If either or both chose to work alone, the individual task operated for both subjects. Whenever a subject switched to "work with other person," a blue light on his partner's panel was illuminated.

In Segment 2 each subject received 6 counts for the individual response and 1 count for cooperation. The segment ended following 135 individual responses by each subject. In Segment 3 these reward magnitudes were reversed. The segment ended following 135 cooperative responses. Completion of these two segments ensured that subjects worked for the larger of two rewards.

In the final 15 minutes of Session 1, subjects worked under the baseline condition. In our initial experiments subjects received 3 counts for cooperating and 2 counts for working individually. Subjects working for 2 counts on the individual task could earn approximately $1.20 per hour— an amount sufficient at that time to maintain participation in the experiment. To compensate for wage inflation, subjects in the later experiments received 4 counts for cooperating and 3 for working individually.

EXPERIMENTAL TREATMENT

Following the training sequence, all experiments followed an intrapair replication procedure in which the effects of the absence or presence of a potentially disruptive treatment were demonstrated for each pair studied (Sidman, 1960). This sequence began in Session 2 with a baseline condition which was identical to that during the training sequence. Subjects could either cooperate or work individually, with cooperation paying 1 count (approximately $.60 per hour) more than individual work. For pairs that did not cooperate under the initial conditions, an additional period was run in which the difference in rewards between cooperation and individual work was increased to 2 counts (approximately $1.20 per hour). In order that any disruption of cooperation caused by the treatment would be apparent, only pairs that cooperated at a high rate during one of the above baseline conditions were studied further. Noncooperative subjects were considered to find the reward differences insufficient to motivate cooperation, and thus not appropriate for the questions of interest. This lack of responsiveness to reward differences occurred very rarely.

For the pairs who cooperated during the baseline condition, one of the potentially disruptive treatments was then introduced. The condition was left in effect for a length of time sufficient to permit a stable response pattern to develop. In longitudinal studies using response rates, the introduction of a new condition has often been found to produce a period of adaptation for subjects in which they explore the new contingencies. Thus, behavior patterns that appear initially are often unstable, and may bear little resemblance to ones that develop later.

Finally, the baseline conditions were reinstated. For pairs that ceased cooperating under the treatment, re-emergence of cooperation in the baseline condition suggests that the treatment, not time, was responsible for the change in behavior. In many cases the baseline–treatment—baseline-sequence was repeated several times, with subjects returning to the laboratory for as many as 12 hours over 6 days.

ANALYSIS

The basic unit of analysis was not individual behavior but the presence or absence of the more complex social response—cooperation. In each experiment the intrapair replication procedures described above permitted us to assess the disruptive effects of a given treatment for each pair. The primary analysis thus focused on the common behavior patterns which developed.

In order to permit a comparison of the size of the effects of the various disruptive conditions, we also report two different summary measures for each experiment. Both of these measures focus on the eventual, or long-term effects, rather than on the initial effects of a given condition. We assume that the subjects' behavior at the conclusion of a condition represents a more reliable and also more conservative estimate of that condition's effect.

Since our primary concern is the extent to which a condition disrupts cooperation, the simplest measure with which conditions can be compared is the proportion of pairs which are cooperating at the conclusion of the potentially disruptive condition. A pair is categorized as cooperative if the percentage of cooperative responses during the final 30 minutes under the disruptive condition is at least 80% that during the baseline condition. A 20% reduction in cooperation for a 30-minute period constitutes a statistically significant change in percentage, given at least a moderate overall rate of response.[2] In fact, how-

---

[2]($p < .01$), test for difference between independent proportions (McNemar, 1969, p. 62). Although the two proportions compared are otained from the same pair, the proportions themselves are based on separate behavior samples usually of different size. The test for differences between nonindependent proportions is not applicable under these conditions.

ever, pairs were typically either wholly cooperative or non-cooperative at the conclusion of a condition.

The other comparative measure is an overall estimate of the variance in the proportion of cooperative responses explained by the presence of a given condition. For each experiment, the proportion of cooperative responses for each pair during the baseline segments was compared with the proportion during the final 30 minutes of the disruptive condition to calculate a point biserial correlation coefficient (eta). The estimate of the percentage of variance in cooperation which that condition explains for the sample of pairs as a whole is eta^2. The size of eta^2 is a function both of the mean difference in proportion of cooperative responses during the periods with and without the disruptive condition, and of the variability in response among the individual pairs within the sample. Explained variance estimates approaching 100% indicate almost complete disruption of cooperation by a given condition, while estimates near 0% indicate little disruption.

CHAPTER 3

THE FIRST EXPERIMENTS:
INEQUITY AND COOPERATION

This chapter reports on a series of experiments which concern differences in the comparative magnitude of rewards for cooperation. We began by studying reward inequity primarily because a prior literature had developed regarding its effects. As will become apparent, however, the conditions relevant to the effects of inequity and inter-personal risk are not discrete. One inequity experiment also contained our first manipulation of risk as part of our treatment of the ability to transfer rewards.

Inequity Size and Withdrawal from Cooperation

The first three experiments investigated the effects of inequity size on the likelihood of withdrawal from cooperation. The major difference among the experiments was the size of the reward inequity for work on the cooperative task. We studied the effects first of a "small," then of a "moderate," and finally of a "large" inequity. Although the time which elapsed between experiments necessitated a change in the rewards for the large inequity experiment, our analysis will consider the three simultaneously.

All experiments began with both subjects able to earn more money by cooperating than by working individually. The rewards for both subjects were equal. Inequity was then introduced by arbitrarily raising the rewards of one of the subjects when both were cooperating. Thus, when the two subjects were cooperating, they were receiving unequal amounts for the same work, but more than they could by working alone. When working alone, both subjects received equal amounts, which were less than they could earn by working together.

The major dependent variable was the proportion of responses which were cooperative under these conditions. Since all subjects preferred more money to less and worked on the cooperative task prior to the introduction of unequal—and hence inequitable—rewards, any work on the individual task reflected an economically "irrational" response to inequity. To further demonstrate that inequity was the source of these departures from cooperation, the original equity conditions were repeated to see whether pairs would again cooperate (reversal).

An important consequence of the investigation of the effects of inequity size on cooperation is the clarification of its impact as an aversive stimulus. The aversiveness of inequity would be most clearly confirmed if withdrawal from cooperation (by either the overpaid or underpaid subjects) increased as the size of inequity increased. On the other hand, the concommitant increase in rewards for the overpaid subjects as the inequity is increased may produce the opposite relationship if the inequity effects are weak. An underpaid subject may choose to deny his partner inequitable earnings when the gain is small but not when it is large. In addition, the overpaid subject may be willing to give up small, but not large, gains to produce equity.

After the effects of inequity on withdrawal were determined, subjects in the moderate inequity experiment participated in two additional sessions, during which they were allowed to transfer rewards. The effect of this treatment on cooperation is described in a separate section later in this chapter.

METHOD

Twenty-one pairs of subjects were studied in both the small and moderate inequity experiments. Ten pairs were studied in the large inequity experiment. In each experiment, half of the pairs were male and half were female.

The setting, subject recruitment and training procedures were those described in detail in Chapter 2. All subjects were scheduled for two 2-hour sessions in addition to the training session (Session 1.) The sequence of conditions is shown in Table 3-1. Session 2 began with 15 minutes of an equity baseline condition to determine if a high rate of cooperation (defined as at least two-thirds of the time spent on the cooperative task) would result with a 1-count reward difference favoring cooperation. For the small and moderate inequity experiments, each cooperative response earned three counts and each individual response 2 counts. For the large inequity experiment run later, the

Table 3-1

Conditions Defining Inequity Experiments with College Students

Session	Segment	Inequity experiment	Cooperation A	B	Individual A and B	Minutes in segment
1	1–4	Training (See Chapt. 2, Table 2-1)				
2	5	Equity baseline				
		Small and moderate	3	3	2	15
		Large	4	4	3	
	6	Inequity				
		Small	6	3	2	90
		Moderate	9	3	2	
		Large	20	4	3	
3	7	Inequity				
		Small	6	3	2	90
		Moderate	9	3	2	
		Large	20	4	3	
	8	Inequity baseline				
		Small and moderate	3	3	2	15
		Large	4	4	3	
		Moderate inequity				
4	9	Equity baseline	3	3	2	15
	10	Inequity with transfer	9	3	2	90
5	11	Inequity with transfer	9	3	2	90
	12	Equity baseline	3	3	2	15

The "Counts[a]" header spans the Cooperation (A, B) and Individual A and B columns.

[a] Each count was worth .1¢

cooperative and individual earnings were 4 and 3 counts respectively.

The equity baseline was included despite an identical one during the training session to ensure that the subjects were under the control of the reward contingencies at the time of the initiation of inequitable conditions. If a high rate of cooperation was not achieved under equity baseline conditions, an additional 15-minute segment was run with the reward for cooperation raised 1 count, producing a 2-count difference between the cooperative and individual tasks. If cooperation was not achieved during the second segment, yet a third was attempted with conditions identical to the second segment.[1] Pairs failing to cooperate during the third segment were not studied further. Thus, all pairs who continued for the remainder of the sessions cooperated for either a 1-count or 2-count difference favoring cooperation. The reward magnitudes under which a pair cooperated defined its equity baseline for the remainder of the experiment.

Session 2 concluded with a 90-minute segment under one of the three inequity conditions. In each experiment Subject B continued to receive the baseline amount for cooperation. As shown in Table 3-1, Subject A received two, three, or five times as much as Subject B for each cooperative response under the small, moderate, or large variations, respectively. No instructions accompanied the introduction of inequity, although the amounts did appear on the television screen.

Session 3 began with a 90-minute inequity segment with rewards identical to those used in the previous session, and concluded with a 15-minute equity baseline segment.

[1]Two pairs in the small inequity experiment cooperated with the 2-count difference.

RESULTS

Fifty of the 52 pairs reached the training and baseline criteria. One pair in the moderate inequity experiment failed to complete the training segments in two attempts, and one pair in the small inequity experiment failed to cooperate during the baseline segments. Neither pair was studied further.

Equity Baseline Conditions. The effects of inequity on cooperation were determined by comparing each pair's cooperative and individual behavior under equity conditions (baseline periods) with its own behavior under conditions of inequity. The behavior of pairs during the equity baseline segments supports the assumption that in the absence of inequity, cooperation accompanied by higher rewards will be selected over individual work at a lower rate of pay. For all 50 pairs (three experiments combined) the proportion of responses which were cooperative was extremely high. With three exceptions, at least 85% of every pair's responses were cooperative. In the three exceptions, at least 70% of the responses were cooperative. The mean was 96%. Response rates were typically at or near the maximum—from 9 to 10 cooperative responses per minute.

No control group was run in which pairs worked under equity baseline conditions over long periods of time. The replicability of the high rates of cooperation in the baseline segments despite intervening conditions that could disrupt cooperation suggests that preference for the higher-paying task is not affected by time. Most departures from cooperation in baseline conditions occurred early in the first baseline segment—when subjects explored the alternatives. Whatever effects boredom or other random factors had were not evident after relatively long periods of time.

Inequity and Withdrawal. To answer the question as to whether or not inequity can disrupt cooperation, the most relevant results are from the large inequity experiment where the most severely inequitable conditions were imposed. The results clearly support the proposition that inequity of at least this amount is aversive for some subjects, and they will withdraw from the inequitable task. In each inequity experiment, withdrawal by a pair was judged to have occurred if individual responses throughout the two inequity periods increased more than 15% over the baseline percentage. Such a difference was also statistically significant.[2]

As Table 3-2 shows, four of the 10 pairs (all female) withdrew entirely from cooperation for very substantial periods under the large inequity. Three of these eventually withdrew totally. In each there was no cooperation at all during the inequity segment of Session 3 and little or no

Table 3-2

Summary of Effects: Inequity Experiments

Pattern	Large inequity		Moderate inequity		Small inequity	
	n	%	*n*	%	*n*	%
Undisrupted cooperation	6	60	15	75	17	85
Mixed cooperation/ noncooperation	1	10	2	10	3	15
Eventual total noncooperation	3	30	3	15	0	0
Total:	10	100	20	100	20	100

[2]$p < .01.$, test for differences between independent proportions.

cooperation in Session 2. Overall, the three pairs worked individually on 100, 97, and 97% of their responses, respectively. Thus, each pair sacrificed at least 1,700 opportunities to earn more money in order to avoid inequity. This meant a loss of approximately $1.70 for the underpaid subject and a loss of $28.90 for her favored partner. The fourth disrupted pair worked individually on 51% of its responses. Most of the individual responses were made during Session 3. The subjects sacrificed approximately $1.00 and $17.00, respectively, by avoiding the inequitable rewards. Among the nondisrupted pairs, no more than 1% of the responses were individual.

The results of the small and moderate inequity experiments indicate that the effects of inequity on cooperation are a function of the size of that inequity. Table 3-2 shows that the proportion of pairs with at least some noncooperation declined from 40% under large inequity to 25% under moderate inequity and 15% under small inequity. As the size of the inequity decreased, the length of the disruption of cooperation also tended to decrease. Pairs showing some noncooperation under moderate and small inequity typically worked only intermittently on the individual task rather than withdrawing totally. No pairs under small inequity and only two pairs under moderate inequity (both female) were noncooperative at the conclusion of the inequity condition. Pairs who withdrew under large inequity worked individually for an average of 86% of their responses; under moderate inequity the average was 50% (range: 18–100%), and under small inequity the average was 39% (range: 26–51%). For the underpaid subject in the moderate inequity experiment withdrawal meant an average sacrifice of approximately $.85 to avoid inequity, while his overpaid partner lost almost $6.00. In the small inequity experiment the comparable losses were approximately $.75 and $1.50. Among the nondisrupted pairs, no more than 8% of the responses were individual.

The variance in the proportion of cooperative responses explained by inequity during the final 30 minutes of the inequity condition was 23% for large inequity (means: baseline .98, inequity .62), 10% for moderate inequity (means: baseline .98, inequity .84), and 7% for small inequity (means: baseline .94, inequity .97). Since the proportion of cooperative responses under small inequity is slightly higher than under baseline conditions, that variance estimate obviously cannot be interpreted as evidence of disruption. Note that by including only the data from the end of the inequity conditions, the variance estimates do not include the transitory effects of inequity which were observed in some pairs who initially spent periods working individually.

In each of the disrupted pairs in the large and moderate inequity experiments, withdrawal from cooperation was initiated by the underpaid subject who thus prevented his partner from earning the larger inequitable amounts. In the small inequity experiment, however, the disruption was initiated by the overpaid subject in two of the three disrupted pairs.

Examination of the rates of cooperation for subjects who remained cooperative under inequity indicated that high rates of cooperation continued. That is, underpaid subjects did not prevent their overpaid partners from obtaining the larger rewards either by switching to cooperation and failing to pull the plunger or by pulling in a desultory manner. In none of the pairs were there any noticeable periods of noncooperation. All subjects either cooperated or worked individually at high rates.

Inequity, Reward Transfers, and Cooperation

In the experimental conditions described above, subjects could make only a single relevant behavioral response to inequity—withdrawal from cooperation. Several studies of the effects of inequity on behavior have indicated that when permitted to do so, subjects will transfer rewards toward equity as an alternative behavioral response (Blumstein & Weinstein, 1969; Leventhal, Allen, & Kemelgor, 1969; Leventhal, Weiss, & Long, 1969; Leventhal & Bergman, 1969; Leventhal & Anderson, 1970). In other words, subjects who are overpaid will give some of their rewards to their underpaid partners. This transfer of rewards is often an alternative outside the laboratory, where side payments cannot be prevented. The opportunity to transfer might be particularly relevant in a cooperative situation where the overpaid subject is dependent upon his underpaid partner for his high rewards.

The effects of the opportunity to transfer rewards on rate of cooperation were studied using the subjects who had participated earlier in the moderate inequity experiment. The decision to study the effects of transfers came after completion of the small inequity experiment, thus prohibiting the use of those subjects. Under large inequity conditions transfer was not feasible due to the limitations of the means of transfer used. A button press was required for each count transferred. Subjects in several large inequity pairs we investigated were physically unable to both cooperate efficiently and transfer to equity (requiring approximately 75 responses per minute). Hence, the restriction of the research to the moderate inequity subjects.

The effects of transfer were investigated in two sessions. In both of these, moderate inequity was retained, but the subjects were also given the opportunity to reallocate rewards. In half the pairs each subject was given a button which gave 1 count to his partner each time it was pressed. In the other 10 pairs each subject was given a button which took 1 count from his partner. The procedure permitted the transfer of as much as $17.00 (all of the overpaid subject's earnings) in the two sessions.

These "rectifiable" inequity conditions provided evidence bearing on several questions. First, if an under-paid subject responds initially to inequity by withdrawal, will his partner attempt to prevent further withdrawal by transferring money to produce equity? Second, will a subject who does not withdraw initially from inequity subsequently withdraw if his partner fails to rectify the inequity through transfers? Third, does the mode of transfer, that is, giving or taking, affect the likelihood that equity or cooperation will be achieved?

METHOD

The sequence of conditions in Session 4 and 5 is shown in Table 3-1. Following an initial 15-minute equity baseline in Session 4, each subject in half of the 20 pairs was provided with a panel button (previously covered) programmed to allow him to give the other some of his money. Subjects received the following instructions over the intercom:

> *Each of you has a button which you can press to give the other person .1¢ of your money. Each time you press the button, you give the other person .1¢.*

Each subject was instructed to press the button several times to observe its function. A subject could use the button any time during the segment as long as he had money to transfer.

Each subject in the other half of the pairs was provided with the same button, now programmed to allow him to take money from the other when both had chosen to cooperate. Subjects received the following instructions:

> *Each of you now has a button which you can press to take money from the other person. Each time you press the*

button you take .1 ¢ from the other person and give .1 ¢ to yourself. Both of you turn your switches to "work with the other person." Notice that the yellow light next to the "take money" button is on.

After each subject pressed his button several times, subjects were shown that the take button was on only when both had chosen to cooperate.

Both of you turn your switches to "work alone." As you see, the light shows that the "take money" button is now off. The button is off whenever either one or both of you switch to "work alone." It is on only when you both switch to "work with the other person."

This contingency allowed a subject to avoid unwanted loss if he chose not to cooperate. When cooperation was the mutual choice, a subject could use the button at any time as long as the other subject had any money. Session 4 concluded with a 90-minute inequity segment with one of the two transfer buttons available. Session 5 began with a 90-minute inequity segment with transfer and ended with a 15-minute baseline segment. During the inequity segments, the yellow light next to the transfer button was illuminated, while during the baseline segments the button and light were covered.

RESULTS

Results from both the giving and taking variations indicate greater response to moderate inequity than when withdrawal alone was possible. Three different types of response emerged: noncooperation, transfer of money and cooperation, or noncooperation followed by transfer and cooperation. Transfer of money was judged to have occurred whenever the subjects reduced the cooperation-induced differences in rewards by at least 50%. Net transfers which met this criterion ranged from $2.51 to $7.61. Within each transferring pair, the underpaid subject received a greater proportion of the money transferred. Combining giving and taking variations, 17 of the 20 pairs (85%) showed some response to inequity (Table 3-3). In other words, inequity with the opportunity to transfer clearly evoked some response in most pairs.

Table 3-3

Summary of Effects: Moderate Inequity with a Means of Transfer

| | Type of Transfer | | | |
| | Give | | Take | |
Pattern	n	%	n	%
Undisrupted cooperation and no transfer	1	10	2	20
Undisrupted cooperation and transfer	4	40	3	30
Noncooperation followed by transfer and cooperation	3	30	4	40
Mixed cooperation/ noncooperation and no transfer	1	10		
Eventual total noncooperation and no transfer	1	10	1	10
Total:	10	100	10	100

Giving Variation. Nine of the 10 pairs in the giving variation made some response to inequity. A comparison of each pair's behavior under rectifiable and nonrectifiable inequity indicates that the opportunity to transfer both facilitated cooperation in previously non-cooperative pairs and produced some noncooperation in previously cooperative pairs if no transfers were made. In two of the three pairs who had shown some noncooperation under nonrectifiable inequity, an initial period of non-cooperation was followed by transfer and cooperation. In both pairs the overpaid subject gave little or no money early in the segment, while his underpaid partner worked intermittently on the individual task. Once the overpaid partner began to give money, the pairs cooperated fully. The third previously noncooperative pair eventually cooperated without any transfer.

Of the seven cooperative pairs under nonrectifiable inequity, four transferred substantial amounts of money while continuing to cooperate. Two pairs showed some noncooperation but did not transfer any substantial amounts. In one of these pairs subjects worked individually on 17% of their responses while in the other the under-paid subject quit midway through the last session after having cooperated throughout most of the previous ses-sion while receiving less than $.04 in transfers. Finally, one pair cooperated with transfer following an intial period of noncooperation. For the sample as a whole, inequity with the opportunity to give money explained 10% of the vari-ance in the proportion of cooperative responses (means: baseline .99, inequity .84).

Taking Variation. Eight of the 10 pairs in the taking variation made some response to inequity. As in the giving variation, the opportunity to transfer facilitated cooperation in previously cooperative pairs and produced some noncooperation in previously cooperative pairs who failed to transfer. In both previously noncooperative pairs, a period of noncooperation was followed by cooperation with transfer. Of the eight previously cooperative pairs, three transferred while continuing to cooperate, two cooperated with transfer following noncooperation, and one was noncooperative and did not transfer. Subjects in the noncooperative pair worked individually on 58% of their responses and were noncooperative at the conclusion of the condition. For the sample as a whole, inequity with the opportunity to take money explained 1% of the variance in the proportion of cooperative responses (means: baseline .94, inequity .91).

Taking, Inequity, and Cooperation. One of the important characteristics differentiating taking from giving as a mode of transfer is that taking is rewarding regardless of whether one is ahead or behind. Availability of taking might therefore be expected to result in conflict as well as transfer. The data bear this out. When giving was available, it was used almost exclusively by the overpaid subject. The most given by any underpaid subject was $.26. This was not the case when taking was the mode of transfer. Seven of the 10 overpaid subjects took at least $.26 and three of them took more than $1.00. It is important to note, however, that in only one of these pairs did the overpaid subject finish with a net gain from the taking, and five of the pairs showed substantial transfers to the underpaid subject by the end of the experiment. For all five of these pairs, the pattern was one of bilateral taking during the first hour followed by little or no taking by the overpaid subject for the remainder of the inequity period. During this time the overpaid subject clearly permitted his partner to rectify the inequity.

Sex Differences. Experimental research in various settings suggests that in general females are somewhat less cooperative than males and more likely to avoid interpersonal situations entailing risk (Kelley, 1965). Combining the data from the three variations suggests that this is also the case here. Of the 12 pairs who showed at least some noncooperation during nonrectifiable conditions, 10 were female—a statistically significant difference.[3] Under rectifiable conditons, seven of the nine pairs evidencing substantial noncooperation were female. With the smaller N, however, this difference was not statistically significant.

A Replication with Children

One of the basic and inevitable criticisms of laboratory research is that it uses highly selected pools of subjects rather than meaningful "samples." Consequently, the findings lack external validity (Campbell & Stanley, 1963) beyond the very constricted specifics of the original setting and procedures. Thus, as with some of the findings reported later in this book (see Chapter 5), we took advantage of an opportunity to replicate the relationship between inequity and cooperation with a different sample.

The sample consisted of children between the ages of 9 and 12. These subjects were particularly interesting with regard to the question as to when equity norms develop. Assuming that the response of any individual to inequity is the product of complex learning experiences, when in the socialization process do these responses come into play? Will inequity in a cooperative context be similarly disruptive for children as for adults?

Most research testing the equity propositions has been conducted only with adults. Exceptions are studies of reward allocation by Leventhal and Anderson (1970) with kindergarten children and by Lerner (1974) with kindergarten, first-grade, and fifth-grade children. The results from both studies indicate that at least some children distribute rewards in proportion to relative performance when their work is either superior or inferior to that of a

[3]$p < .05., x^2$ test.

partner. In the present setting, withdrawal from cooperation has far more drastic consequences than reward allocation in terms of both the disruption of the relationship
and the potential monetary loss or gain.

METHOD

Twelve pairs of children ages 9 to 12 were studied. This
age range was selected after preliminary investigation
revealed that children as young as 9 could learn to cooperate
at a high rate in our setting. Six of the pairs were male and
six were female. In addition, half of these pairs were siblings and half were strangers. In studying siblings, we were
interested in finding whether inequity would affect
cooperation between partners who had close prior relations
and could interact between inequity sessions. The sequence
of conditions is shown in Table 3-4. With the following
exceptions, the procedures were similar to those of the small
inequity experiment. Instructions during training were
simplified and the experimenter's demonstration of the
task was more extensive. Each training segment was

Table 3-4

Conditions Defining Inequity Experiment with Children

Session		Segment	Counts[a]		Individual A and B	Minutes in segment
			Cooperation A	B		
1	1-4	Training				
2	5	Equity baseline	2	2	1	15
	6	Inequity	4	2	1	45
3	7	Inequity	4	2	1	45
	8	Equity baseline	2	2	1	15

[a]Each count was worth .1¢.

shortened so that the sequence during Session 1 was completed within approximately 1 hour. Because of the possibility of less proficiency among children in the cooperative task, no prespecified criterion of cooperation was used during the first equity baseline. In Sessions 2 and 3, baseline segments were 15 minutes, and inequity segments 45 minutes in length.

In the equity baseline, subjects received 2 counts for cooperating and 1 count for working individually. During inequity, the overpaid subject's reward for cooperating was increased to 4 counts. In each pair the younger of the two children was always the overpaid. This prevented the subjects from interpreting the reward discrepancy as an equitable return for age difference. At the upper limit of task efficiency, the overpaid subject in a fully cooperative pair could earn approximately $2.10 per session, and the underpaid subject $1.05.

RESULTS

The behavior of the children under equity and inequity closely paralleled that of the college students, supporting the proposition that equity norms are learned early. Ten of the 12 pairs cooperated on at least 83% of their responses during the equity baseline segments. The remaining two pairs cooperated on 53% and 48% of their responses, respectively. As Table 3-5 shows, five of the 12 pairs showed some withdrawal from cooperation during inequity. Two of the pairs were noncooperative at the end of the final inequity segment. Overall, inequity explained 12% of the variance in the proportion of cooperative responses (means: baseline .88, inequity .67).

Inequity had a somewhat greater effect on cooperation of strangers than of siblings. Of the nonsibling pairs, three (all female) were significantly less cooperative under inequity than equity. Except for four cooperative responses, one pair worked only individually under inequity. For the other two pairs, the proportion of cooperative responses during equity and inequity decreased from 100 to 32% and from 99 to 68%, respectively. Two sibling pairs (one male and one female) were significantly less cooperative under inequity than equity. These were also the two pairs who were least cooperative during the equity segments. For the female pair, the percentage of cooperative responses decreased from 53 during equity to 27 during inequity. For the male pair, the decrease was from 48 to 21%.

In each of the disrupted pairs withdrawal from cooperation was initiated by the underpaid subject. This was the same pattern previously observed for college students in the moderate and large inequity variations. Unexpectedly, postexperimental questioning of the siblings did not reveal any exchanges, agreements, or threats made between sessions. However, the children typically did not respond at any length to the questions and may not have related more subtle influence attempts.

Table 3-5

Summary of Effects: Children under Inequity

Pattern	Siblings		Strangers	
	n	%	*n*	%
Undisrupted cooperation	4	67	3	50
Mixed cooperation/ noncooperation	2	33	2	33
Eventual total noncooperation			1	17
Total:	6	100	6	100

Conclusion

The results clearly demonstrate that for a substantial minority of subjects inequity can destroy cooperation. In particular, some underpaid subjects are willing to forego the greater rewards produced by cooperation if they are accompanied by inequity. The likelihood of withdrawal appears to be greatest if the overpaid subject can permit transfer of rewards but refuses to do so. When the inequitable differences are small some overpaid subjects will forego additional rewards to produce equity.

The likelihood and severity of the disruption of cooperation increased with increasing degrees of inequity. In one sense, withdrawal as a response to large inequity was more "irrational" than a similar response to small inequity since inequity was produced by increasing the total amount of reward available to the pair. Thus, by withdrawing from cooperation the pair as a whole was giving up much more money to avoid inequity under large than under small inequity conditions.

It should also be noted that the amount of inequity experienced by the subjects under this design accumulated over time. For college students the number of task behaviors enacted (approximately 4,800) and the amount of time spent by each subject (from 6 to 10 hours) were both unusually large for laboratory research. Still, they have not been enough to allow for the full impact of inequity on behavior. These limitations may account for the fact that although cooperation was severely disrupted in some pairs, the majority of pairs remained cooperative under non-rectifiable inequity. It is reasonable to postulate the accumulation of resentment over "unfair treatment" which, for some individuals, finally reaches a threshold only after several years. It may only be at this point that an employee, for example, commences "irrational" slowdowns or sabotage of his "cooperative" work environment. In this regard, Adams hypothesizes that:

> Leaving the field will be resorted to only when the magnitude of inequity experienced is high and other means of reducing it are unavailable. Partial withdrawal, such as absenteeism, will occur more frequently and under conditions of lower inequity [Adams, 1965, p. 396].

Indeed, the data for moderate and large nonrectifiable inequity conditions indicate that there is more disruption the longer the time spent under the condition, and that the length of each interruption tends to become longer.

When a means of reducing inequity other than withdrawal was provided to the subjects, most of them responded by transferring sufficient amounts to produce partial or total equity. The mode of transfer made available (giving or taking) had little effect on the likelihood that equity and cooperation would be achieved. However, the availability of either means of transfer appeared to increase the likelihood of noncooperation *if no transfers were made.* Underpaid subjects in more than one-third of the pairs who were totally cooperative under nonrectifiable conditions became *less* cooperative when the possibility of transfer was introduced. However, in all cases where noncooperation was followed by substantial transfers, high rates of cooperation resulted.

CHAPTER 4

COOPERATION AND INTERPERSONAL RISK

We turn now to the second variable which frequently accompanies cooperation—the risk of reward loss through expropriation. A hint of its disruptive effects was seen in the previous chapter where conflict, typically short lived, emerged when the opportunity to take was introduced into a cooperative setting with reward inequity. Our concern now will be an investigation of the independent effects of interpersonal risk. Given a situation in which cooperation is equally profitable for all persons, do they cooperate if

57

that activity involves substantial interpersonal risk? Does the opportunity for expropriation produce conflict between partners, destroying cooperation? Or does the very risk of expropriation inhibit any attempt at all at establishing a cooperative effort?

Throughout this research, interpersonal risk is operationally defined as a condition under which each subject may have some or all of his earnings taken or destroyed by the other subject. As in the earlier inequity experiment, a response was added to the basic setting which allowed a subject to take a predetermined amount from the other, but only when the cooperative task had been selected by both subjects. Subjects could choose a safe alternative—the lower-paying individual task—which entailed no risk of expropriation by the other.

It is important to note that despite the interdependence of cooperation and risk, cooperative and taking behaviors were topographically distinct. By selecting the cooperative contingencies, the subjects only made available the cooperative and taking responses. Selecting cooperative conditions did not necessitate the use of either alternative. Subjects could cooperate and not take, take but not cooperate, do both, or do neither. Both behaviors were conditional upon the selection of cooperative conditions, but the two were independent of one another.

Studies in other contexts have suggested the inhibiting effects of risk on cooperation. Risk is an important element in the widely studied "Prisoner's Dilemma" matrix game. In the example shown in Fig. 4-1, Person A's choice of "C," which rewards both players if reciprocated, is termed "cooperative." By selecting the cooperative alternative, however, Person A risks exploitation (A's lowest and B's highest reward) if Person B chooses "D." Under these reward conditions, the majority of subjects begin by trying to exploit their partners but tend to become more cooperative after several hundred trials (Rapaport & Chammah, 1965). These results, however, do not give us an unambiguous picture of the effects of risk on cooperation. First, when a person chooses not to cooperate, it is not clear whether he is trying to exploit his partner or to minimize loss in the face of his partner's exploitation. Second, in the versions of the matrix used most often, cooperation is the only profitable alternative for both subjects in the long run. In this circumstance, cooperation should be especially difficult to eliminate in that any rewarded response is difficult to suppress in the absence of reinforcing alternatives.

Person B

		C	D
	C	1, 1	−2, 2
Person A			
	D	2, −2	−1, −1

Figure 4-1   Typical Prisoner's Dilemma matrix.

An important difference between this and previous research is the difference between expropriation—taking— and competition, the response most often paired with cooperation in previous studies. As generally defined, a situation is competitive if fewer than all persons making some response will be rewarded for it. In the dyadic situation, if one person is rewarded the other is not. In practice, the rewards earned by competing usually originate outside the group of competitors. They are not rewards that one of the competitors has previously earned. Under these conditions competitors may often try to eliminate the uncertainties of competition by converting it to a complex form of cooperation. They may simply make agreements as to who shall perform the rewarded response. For example, what is ostensibly monopolistic competition in major American industries has occasionally been revealed to involve collusion in the form of agreements as to pricing and market share among the "competitors." In contrast to competition, expropriation, that is, taking, transfers rewards which were previously earned. No new rewards are added to the total that the participants have already obtained. Thus taking more closely resembles what in other contexts is termed "stealing."

In this chapter we describe three experiments which establish the basic effect of interpersonal risk on cooperation. Since our interest in risk was provoked by subjects' behavior in the "take" variation of the inequity experiments, we began by repeating that study, but deleting the element of inequity (small-risk experiment). In the second experiment the size of the risk was increased substantially (large-risk experiment). In the third experiment the large-risk condition was run over an extended period of time to test the stability of the risk effect.

The Effects of Interpersonal Risk:
The Small-Risk Experiment

METHOD

Sixteen pairs of male and 17 pairs of female students were scheduled for two sessions. The standard setting and training procedures described in Chapter 2 were used in session 1. Table 4-1 shows the sequence of conditions in Session 2. A baseline without the opportunity to take was followed by a risk condition, in which either subject could take from his partner. The session ended with a return to the original baseline condition.

Table 4-1

Conditions Defining Small- and Large-Risk Experiments

Session	Segment		Counts[a]		Minutes in segment
			Cooperation (each subject)	Individual	
1	1–4	Training			
2	5	Baseline: cooperation or individual reponding	3	2	30[b]
	6	Risk: Cooperation with taking or individual responding	3	2	75
	7	Baseline: cooperation or individual responding	3	2	15

[a]Each count was worth .1¢.

[b]If pair was noncooperative during the first 15 minutes, cooperation paid 4 counts during the last 15 minutes. If pair was noncooperative during the last 15 minutes, baseline was extended an additional 15 minutes with cooperation paying 4 counts.

The initial baseline of Session 2 was longer and employed a more stringent criterion of cooperation than that used in the inequity experiments. All subjects worked at least 30 minutes without the opportunity to take. The baseline sequence began with each subject receiving 3 counts for cooperating and 2 for working individually. If, during the first 15 minutes with the 1-count reward difference, the pair did not cooperate at least 80% of the time, a 2-count difference (cooperation paid 4 counts and individual work paid 2 counts) was used during the second 15 minutes. An additional 15 minutes of the 2-count difference was added if the cooperative criterion was not met by the end of the 30 minutes.[1] Pairs who were cooperative proceeded to the risk segment, while pairs failing to meet the criterion were not studied further.

Before the risk segment, the covers were removed from the take buttons and the subject received instructions identical to those used in the taking variation of the moderate inequity experiment (see Chapter 3). A 75-minute risk period followed. Task rewards for each pair were the same as those used in the baseline. At the end of the 75 minutes, covers were replaced over the take buttons, and a final 15-minute baseline segment was run.

RESULTS

In this and subsequent experiments, analysis of the behavior under the risk conditions was simplified by the fact that most pairs displayed relatively clear and simple patterns of response. Over time a stable pattern of either cooperation or noncooperation typically emerged. In the small-risk experiment only one pair displayed a mixed task pattern with frequent switching from task to task. An illustration of the stability of the behavior of a typical pair is shown in Fig. 4-2. The subjects cooperated at a high rate

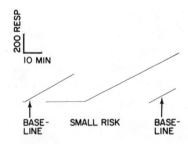

Figure 4-2 Cumulative record of the cooperative responses of one pair during baseline and small-risk conditions. Cooperation reemerged in 21 minutes following the introduction of small risk.

[1]Four pairs worked under this baseline.

during the baseline segments, worked individually at a high rate for 21 minutes following the introduction of risk, then cooperated for the remainder of the session.

All but one of the 33 pairs completed the training and baseline sequence. One pair (male) was noncooperative during the baseline and was not studied further.

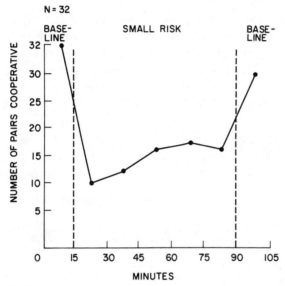

Figure 4-3 Small risk: number of pairs cooperative over time.

Cooperation. Figure 4-3 summarizes the effect of risk by showing the proportion of pairs cooperating (80% of responses cooperative) during 15-minute intervals for the three segments of Session 2. As the figure shows, the introduction of small risk precipitated the loss of cooperation for all but 10 of the 32 pairs which had been cooperating under baseline conditions. However, by the conclusion of the condition, 17 pairs were again cooperative. Twelve of the disrupted pairs were basically noncooperative throughout the entire small-risk segment. An additional 12 pairs were noncooperative for periods ranging from 9 to 34 minutes. For all but three of the latter pairs, the disruption occurred at the beginning of the risk segment and was eventually followed by cooperation. Cooperation resumed in all but two pairs when risk was removed for the final baseline segment. For the sample as a whole, risk explained 25% of the variance in the proportion of cooperative responses (means: baseline .96, risk .56).

Taking and Cooperation. Several different patterns of taking and task behavior emerged under small-risk conditions. However, as Table 4-2 shows, more than two-thirds of the 32 groups fit one of two patterns. The most common pattern involved taking and noncooperation. This pattern is illustrated by pairs B–B and B–S, whose behavior is graphed in Figure 4-4. Both subjects in pair B–B engaged in a number of brief switches to cooperation throughout the segment. However, each switch to cooperation was immediately accompanied by attempts at taking, and no cooperative

Table 4-2

Summary of Effects: Small-Risk Experiment

Pattern	n	%
Eventual cooperation		
Cooperation without taking	6	19
Taking followed by cooperation	9	28
Cooperation and taking	2	6
Eventual noncooperation		
Taking and noncooperation	12	38
Cooperation disrupted by taking	2	6
Mixed cooperation/noncooperation		
Alternating periods of noncooperation and cooperation with taking	1	3
Total:	32	100

behavior occurred. During these occasions both subjects pressed their take buttons at extremely high rates. Whenever one subject began to lose to his partner, the former typically switched to the individual task for a short time. At the conclusion of the small-risk segment one subject had taken 1,210 counts and the other 1,380 counts. Working alone rather than together for the entire period meant that each subject gave up potential earnings of approximately $.75. When risk was terminated the pair returned immediately to a high rate of cooperation. Nine other pairs had patterns of taking and noncooperation approximating that pair of B–B. For two of these, cooperation did not resume when risk was removed. Combined amounts taken in the nine pairs ranged from 110 to 940 counts, whereas within-pair differences in taking ranged from 10 to 400 counts.

In pair B–S, shown in Figure 4-4, taking occurred only during the first part of the small-risk segment. Although both subjects took less than 10 counts during the first 15 minutes of risk, they made no further switches to cooperation until risk was removed. One other pair was similar to B–S; in this pair both subjects took less than 60 counts, yet cooperation did not resume.

The second common response pattern was taking followed by cooperation. Pair A–K in Fig. 4-4 illustrates this pattern. After 21 minutes, during which the subjects took 170 and 140 counts, respectively, taking ceased and cooperation began. Eight other pairs had response patterns similar to A–K. After periods of time ranging from 1 to 34 minutes, each of these pairs stopped taking and began cooperating at a high rate. Total amounts taken in these pairs ranged from 20 to 1,300 counts; within-pair differences ranged from 20 to 160 counts.

A third, less common response to small risk was cooperation without taking. Pair K–N in Fig. 4-4 illustrates this pattern. For this pair, a 3-minute period of work on the

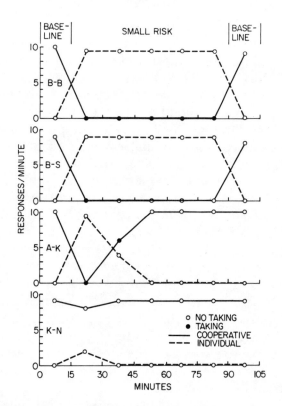

Figure 4-4 Small risk: cooperative and individual response rates and taking patterns for illustrative pairs during 15-minute intervals.

individual task preceded 72 minutes of full cooperation. Four other pairs in which there was no taking, as well as one pair with a single take, followed a similar pattern. In two of these pairs, periods of work on the individual task (3 and 20 minutes, respectively) preceded cooperation. Once cooperation was attempted, however, it was maintained.

The remaining five pairs evidenced three additional response patterns. In two pairs (including the most conflictive) a moderate rate of cooperation continued throughout the session despite frequent taking. In two other pairs cooperation was lost during the risk segment after substantial periods of cooperation (24 and 62 minutes, respectively) when subjects began taking. Finally, one pair switched from one task to the other every few minutes and took frequently while cooperating. In all five of these pairs subjects returned to cooperation when risk was removed.

Sex Differences. Ten of 15 male and seven of 17 female pairs were cooperative by the end of the risk segment. However, females in this setting tended to be more conflictive than males, making significantly greater use of the take buttons.[2]

DISCUSSION

Interpersonal risk produced some behavioral response in most pairs. Three-quarters of the pairs evidenced substantial disruption of cooperation. For half of these disrupted pairs, however, the effect was transitory. Since the return to cooperation usually occurred during the first 35 minutes of the experimental segment, the behavior present at the end of the risk segment had typically been in effect for at least 40 minutes—approximately 400 responses. For all but two noncooperative pairs, disruption ceased when the risk was removed.

Overall, differences in the frequency of taking were extreme. One pair had over 37,000 takes, far more than any other. For most pairs, though, the total number of takes was less than 1,000. Within any pair, the differences between partners in amounts taken was generally small—less than 250 (that is, $.25) in all but two pairs. It should be noted that neither the frequency of takes nor the difference in takes between partners appear to determine

[2] $p < .001$, Mann–Whitney U Test.

whether noncooperation will be temporary or sustained. What is clear, however, is that taking and cooperation are incompatible. Cooperation, if it emerges, typically follows the cessation of all taking.

Increasing Risk's Size: The Large-Risk Experiment

Results of the first risk experiment demonstrated that risk substantially affects the rate of cooperation in at least some cooperating pairs. But is this a fair estimate of the size of the effect that we can expect from risk? This experiment was designed to determine whether amount of disruption is a function of risk size. The amount which could be taken was increased a thousandfold—from $.001 to $1.00.

The results of this experiment were of particular interest in shedding some light on the mechanisms through which risk gains its effects. Several different outcomes appeared plausible. The one which seemed most likely was a further increase in the disruption of cooperation. This would occur if an increase in the rewards for taking makes taking more likely or increases the fear that one's partner will take. It was also possible that the effects of large and small risk would be the same. This outcome would occur if the results of the small-risk experiment were based on the distribution of subjects who were willing to cooperate without taking under risk. Cooperation would occur whenever two cooperatively oriented subjects were paired. Finally, it also seemed possible that an increase in risk might increase cooperation. During the past decade there has been considerable discussion concerning the "flexibility" of a country's defense posture. It has been argued by many that a primary emphasis on nuclear deterrence makes it impossible for a country to fight "limited wars." Without a willingness to deliver a massive blow, force cannot be used. If a country were only very rarely (hopefully never) willing to use nuclear weapons, its ability to coerce other countries would be weakened. Applied to our experiment, such reasoning might argue that the 1,000-count take is too great for subjects to readily use it. Hence, there would actually be much less taking and, consequently, more cooperation.

METHOD

Thirteen male and 15 female pairs were studied for two sessions. With one exception, procedures were the same as those for the small-risk experiment.[3] Each press of the take button now took 1,000 counts ($1.00) from the other person's counter. If the other person had less than 1,000 counts, all but 10 counts were taken. When cooperation was the mutual choice, a subject could take at any time as long as the other subject possessed at least 10 counts.

Subjects received the following instructions before the take segment in Session 2.

> *Each of you now has a button which you can press to take money from the other person. Each time you press the button you take $1 from the other person and give $1 to yourself. If the other person has less than $1, pressing the button will take away almost all of his money, down to about 1¢.*

Each subject then pressed the take button and observed the resulting transfer. Approximately 1 minute was required to transfer 1,000 counts following a press of the take button. During this time the panel light went off, a buzzer sounded continuously, and neither cooperation, individual responding, nor taking was rewarded.

[3]Three pairs required the 2-count difference in task reinforcers before cooperating.

Subjects were then shown that money could be taken only when both had switched to cooperation. The task selection switch remained operative during the transfer of money. Thus, if either subject switched to the individual task during the transfer, the take button would be inoperative when the transfer was completed.

RESULTS AND DISCUSSION

Cooperation. As shown in Fig. 4-5, the effects of large risk on cooperation were extreme. Only two of the 28 pairs were cooperative at the conclusion of the risk condition, a proportion significantly less than under small risk.[4] Twenty-five pairs were noncooperative throughout the entire risk segment, while an additional pair was non-cooperative during the last half of the segment. The marked

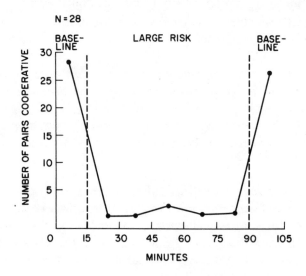

Figure 4-5   Large risk: number of pairs cooperative over time.

[4]$p < .01$, x^2 (two-tailed test).

control over behavior produced by large risk is illustrated by the fact that in 24 pairs not a single cooperative response was made in 75 minutes—and that a twenty-fifth pair cooperated once. Removal of risk conditions led to the resumption of cooperation for all but one of the pairs, although in one other pair the return was not immediate. For the sample as a whole, risk explained 81% of the variance in the proportion of cooperative responses (means: baseline .95, risk .09).

Taking and Cooperation. The introduction of large risk produced a marked similarity in patterns of response. As shown in Table 4-3, all but three of the 28 pairs evidenced periodic taking accompanied by the almost total absence of any cooperative responses.

Taking typically followed a similar pattern. The first take in all but one case occurred in the first 7 minutes under risk. Switches to cooperation by one subject were followed by a nearly simultaneous switch to cooperation with taking by the other, who then switched immediately back to the individual task. Often, subjects who had lost most of their money remained switched to cooperation, attempting (usually unsuccessfully) to take back from a

Table 4-3

Summary of Effects: Large-Risk Experiment

Pattern	n	%
Eventual cooperation		
Cooperation without taking	1	4
Taking followed by cooperation	1	4
Eventual noncooperation		
Taking and noncooperation	25	89
Cooperation disrupted by taking	1	4
Total:	28	101

partner who had employed the previous strategy. This choice involved little cost for the subject who had lost since he could lose no more money than he had accumulated on his counter.

Figure 4-6 shows the number and time of takes by each subject. The total amounts taken by both subjects ranged from 890 to 7,730 counts. Within-pair differences in taking ranged from 0 to 2,900 counts; the median of 920 was approximately 18 times greater than the difference in amount taken under small-risk conditions.

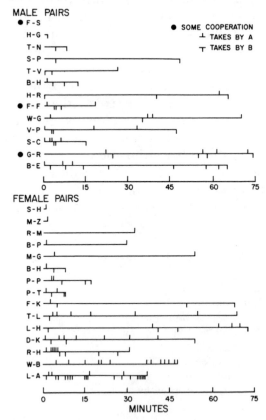

Figure 4-6 Large risk: time of takes by each subject.

Three pairs engaged in some cooperation under risk. One pair experienced no interruption in cooperation following the introduction of risk, and neither subject ever took. In another pair, taking and 21 minutes of work on the individual task were followed by cooperation. In the final pair cooperation was lost after 55 minutes, when subjects began taking frequently. Cooperation resumed when the risk was removed.

Sex Differences. All three of the pairs which had any more than a few cooperative responses were male. As in the previous experiment, females were more conflictive than males, but the difference was not significant.

Durability of the Risk Effect:
The Large-Risk, Extended Experiment

While the markedly disruptive effect of large risk on cooperation was clearly demonstrated in the large-risk experiment, it is possible that the disruption is only transitory. For example, reactions to the persistent loss of potential earnings through noncooperation could increase over longer periods of work, eventually leading pairs to return to cooperation. To examine this possibility, seven pairs were run for additional sessions under large-risk conditions. (Since Session 2 was identical to that in the large-risk experiment, the data for the seven pairs from Session 2 were included in the previous large-risk experiment as well).

METHOD

Three pairs (W–G, T–L, B–P) were studied for a total of four sessions, and four pairs (M–G, W–B, G–R, S–H) were studied for a total of five sessions.

Except for segment lengths and the absence of any further instructions, conditions were identical to those in Session 2. All sessions began with a 30-minute baseline segment in which the take buttons were covered. The risk segment that followed was 60 minutes long in Sessions 3 and 5 and 90 minutes long in Session 4. A final 15-minute baseline segment with the take buttons covered followed the risk segment in Sessions 3 and 5.

RESULTS AND DISCUSSION

The large-risk effect was remarkably stable. Additional time did not increase the amount of cooperation in six of seven pairs. As shown in Table 4-4, only one pair evidenced substantial periods of cooperation during any session. This pair, G–R, cooperated during part of Session 2 and throughout Sessions 3 and 4, but ceased cooperating during the final 8 minutes of Session 5, following a take. This behavior might be a rare instance (in this situation) of the kind of end-game exploitation postulated by Luce and Raiffa (1957) as a basic gaming strategy. Only one other pair had any cooperative responses at all—a total of 13 over the additional hours under these conditions. For the six pairs, risk explained 80% of the variance in the proportion of cooperative responses (means: baseline .98, risk .12).

Table 4-4

Summary of Effects: Large-Risk Extended Experiment

Pattern	n	%
Eventual noncooperation		
Taking and noncooperation	6	86
Cooperation\disrupted by taking	1	14
Total:	7	100

Over a period of time, the six basically noncooperative pairs all evidenced marked decreases in taking. No taking occurred in any of the pairs after Session 3, and in two pairs taking ceased after Session 2. This pattern was primarily a reflection of the increasing unwillingness of most subjects to place themselves under the risk conditions. Five of the seven pairs in Session 4 showed a total avoidance pattern, which none of the 28 pairs evidenced in Session 2. It was the pattern of avoidance (of both risk and cooperation) that apparently was strengthened over time, replacing any tendency to cooperate induced by higher potential earnings. It should also be noted, however, that the removal of risk conditions during baseline segments led repeatedly to the resumption of cooperation.

A NOTE ON "REPLICATIONS" OF THE LARGE-RISK EFFECT

Since the original experiments concerning the large-risk effect, we have run a large number of additional pairs under conditions either identical to or closely resembling those described above. As indicated in succeeding chapters, many of these have involved approximately one-half hour under large-risk conditions as a baseline for other sets of conditions whose effects we wanted to compare. Totaling all of these cases, we find that the basic relation holds. Approximately 80% of all pairs cannot maintain cooperation under large-risk conditions.

Conclusion

Having now concluded three risk experiments, what do we know about the effects of risk on cooperation? First,

cooperation is disrupted by the introduction of interpersonal risk. Disruption is substantial when the risk is
small, almost total when the risk is large. Second, removal
of risk generally leads to the resumption of cooperation.
Third, the effect of large risk on cooperation does not
change substantially with time—at least during approximately 10 hours of experiment time and over a total of at
least 5,000 task responses.

The size and persistence of the risk effect provides
very strong preliminary evidence that the role played by
interpersonal risk may be particularly important in understanding the conditions which lead to the initiation and
disruption of cooperation. Thus, in the following chapter
we attempt to further clarify the effects of risk.

CHAPTER 5

COOPERATION
AND INTERPERSONAL RISK:
TESTS FOR GENERALITY

The large-risk experiments—in essence a series of intrapair replications—provide a strong case for the reliability of the risk effect. However, our findings were also obtained under a very specific set of experimental conditions. Are they limited to this set of conditions alone? Or will they hold under a variety of other circumstances? For example, will the risk effect still be found if the task rewards are changed? If the characteristics of risk are altered? If a

77

different apparatus and procedures are used? If subjects come from a different population? Answers to questions such as these are critical in revealing the generality, and for many the importance, of any effect. Hence, they are our concern in the experiments reported in this chapter.

PART I: VARIATION IN REWARDS

Increasing the Rewards for Cooperation: The Large-Risk, Large-Pay Experiment

In both the large-risk and large-risk extended experiments, a minimal difference favoring cooperation was usually sufficient to induce most pairs to cooperate in the absence of risk. Most subjects cooperated with the 1-count difference in task rewards, thus earning approximately $.60 more per hour than when they worked individually. But to what extent is the disruptive effect of risk limited to this small reward difference? Outside the laboratory the advantages which lead people to cooperate are usually much more than minimal. If the risk effect were limited to overcoming only small differences, its generality would be restricted indeed. Thus, we designed this experiment to test the risk effect against more substantial differences in task rewards. The cooperative reward was increased from 3 to 9 counts per response, while the individual task reward remained at two counts. With the resultant difference, each subject could earn approximately $4.20 per hour more working cooperatively than he could by working on the individual task.

METHOD

Five female and four male pairs were scheduled for three sessions in the standard setting. The sequence of con-

Table 5-1

Conditions Defining Large-Risk, Large-Pay Experiment

Session	Segment		Counts[a]		Minutes in segment
			Cooperation (each subject)	Individual	
1	1–4	Training			
2	5	Baseline: co-operation or individual responding	3	2	30
	6	Risk: cooper-ation with taking or individual responding	9	2	75
	7	Baseline: cooperation or individual responding	3	2	15
3	8	Baseline	3	2	30
	9	Risk	9	2	60
	10	Risk	3	2	15

[a]Each count was worth .1¢.

ditions is shown in Table 5-1.[1] Instructions were identical to those used in the large-risk experiment. As the table shows, the cooperative reward of 3 counts during the baseline segments was increased to 9 counts during all but the last risk segment. During the last 15 minutes of Session 3, risk remained, but the cooperative reward was set at 3 (rather than 9) counts to determine if pairs who cooperated with the higher amount would cease to cooperate when the amount was reduced.

[1]One pair required the 2-count difference in task rewards before cooperating.

RESULTS AND DISCUSSION

Increasing the magnitude of the reward for cooperation reduced but did not eliminate the substantial effect
of risk. With the large earnings, only 3 of the 9 pairs (two
male, one female) were cooperative at the end of final risk
segment. For the sample as a whole, risk explained 43% of
the variance in the proportion of cooperative responses
(means: baseline .93, risk .33).

Patterns of disruption (Table 5-2) were similar to those
occurring with the smaller differences in earnings. As in
prior experiments, most takes occurred during the first
15 minutes of risk conditions and decreased over time. One
of the three cooperative pairs ceased cooperating when
the large rewards were no longer present in the final
risk segment.

Table 5-2

Summary of Effects: Large-Risk, Large-Pay Experiment

Pattern	n	%
Eventual cooperation		
Cooperation without taking	1	11
Taking followed by cooperation	2	22
Eventual noncooperation		
Taking and noncooperation	5	56
Cooperation disrupted by taking	1	11
Total:	9	100

The small effect of a threefold increase in cooperative
earnings emphasizes more strongly the behavioral control
over cooperation exerted by the ability to take. It still seems
reasonable, however, that reward differences could be
specified which would be sufficient to decrease substan-

tially the disruptive effect of risk. Results from this experiment, however, suggest that these differences must be very large.

Eliminating the Rewards for Taking: The Destroy Experiment

Although we have demonstrated that interpersonal risk tends to disrupt cooperation, we have not fully specified the characteristic of risk central to this effect. As an interpersonal behavior, taking has more than one consequence—a positive one for the taker and a negative one for the person taken from. Thus, risk could produce noncooperation in several ways, even within a given pair. First, subjects could eschew cooperation primarily as a means of protecting themselves from loss. Second, noncooperation could be the result of taking. Because of the large and immediate reward involved, taking might be the preferred first response. Subjects may then choose the individual task primarily to protect their gains or to avoid further loss.

Both of these explanations rely on the reward contingencies, which we have assumed are the salient ones governing behavior in the risk setting. However, there is the possibility that these intended consequences are not the only ones in our experimental procedure. It has been suggested that subjects in experimental situations may engage in various behaviors simply because they are available, or because of the "demand characteristics" of the experiment (Rosenthal, 1966; Webb *et al.*, 1966; Wiggins, 1968). Thus it can be argued that subjects may be expected to press the take button, thereby initiating conflict and eventual noncooperation. Taking occurs simply because the button is present, or because the experimenter's demonstration of its function is interpreted as a direction to use it. Data from the previous risk experiments suggest that for most pairs the risk–avoidance pattern becomes important only after a period of conflict. This indicates that at least intially taking is predominant in producing noncooperation. The data, however, tell us nothing about what motivates the taking.

We designed an experiment to answer the question of motivation. For this purpose, the element of reward was divorced from the element of risk. Simply stated, this experiment was identical to the large-risk experiment, except that a press of the "take" button garnered *no* rewards for the taker. It still removed $1 of the other person's money, but it added nothing to the taker's total. Thus the "risk" of losing money remained. By cooperating, a subject still exposed himself to a reduction in his earnings. If subjects did *not* use the take button under these destroy conditions, it would be clear that rewards, not "demand characteristics," produced taking.

METHOD

Five female and three male pairs were studied for three sessions in the standard setting. The sequence of conditions is shown in Table 5-3. Unlike the large-risk experiment, each press of the take button resulted only in the reduction of the other person's earnings by 1,000 counts, or all but 10 counts of his earnings if he had less than 1,000. The word "destroy" was substituted for the word "take" throughout the risk instructions.

RESULTS AND DISCUSSION

As Table 5-4 shows, the opportunity to destroy $1 of the other person's earnings produced no disruption in the majority of the pairs. Cooperation was totally disrupted in only one male pair. In two other pairs cooperation was dis-

Table 5-3

Conditions Defining Destroy Experiment

Session		Segment	Cooperation (each subject)	Individual	Minutes in segment
			Counts[a]		
1	1–4	Training			
2	5	Baseline: cooperation or individual responding	3	2	30
	6	Risk–Destroy: cooperation with destroy or individual responding	3	2	75
	7	Baseline: cooperation or individual responding	3	2	15
3	8	Baseline	3	2	30
	9	Risk–Destroy	3	2	60
	10	Baseline	3	2	15

[a]Each count was worth .1¢.

Table 5-4

Summary of Effects: Large-Risk Destroy Experiment

Pattern	n	%
Eventual cooperation		
Cooperation without destroying	5	62
Delayed cooperation without destroying	2	25
Eventual noncooperation		
Destroying and noncooperation	1	12
Total:	8	99

rupted for shorter periods of time—one throughout the first destroy segment and the other for a 21-minute period early in the first destroy segment. At the conclusion of the destroy condition all but one of the pairs (male) were cooperative, a proportion significantly greater than under large risk.[2] For the sample as a whole the opportunity to destroy explained 6% of the variance in the proportion of cooperative responses (means: baseline .98, destroy .86).

Most important, only one of the 16 subjects ever used the destroy button. This subject, a member of the totally noncooperative pair, destroyed earnings three times during Session 2. Thus it appears reasonable to assume that subjects in previous experiments did not press the take buttons either simply because they were present or because they were shown how to do so. Instead, they pressed because of the reinforcing consequences of that behavior.

PART II: VARYING OTHER CHARACTERISTICS OF RISK

The Effects of Scheduling: The Intermittent Availability of Risk Experiment

In the risk experiments reported to this point, the opportunity to take was always available whenever both subjects chose to cooperate. Such continuous availability, however, is only one of many "schedules" with which risk can be present. Risk can also be intermittent in an almost infinite variety of patterns. As with our choice of reward magnitudes, the continuous risk variation studied thus far

---

[2] $p < .005$, Fisher Exact Probability Test. In this and all subsequent analyses, one-tailed tests were used.

is probably not the most common one outside the laboratory. In fact, a glance at most consequences commonly experienced in everyday life suggests that few result every time a given behavior is performed.

Following the work of Ferster and Skinner (1957), psychologists have catalogued a variety of important effects that the schedule of a consequence can have on the response patterns of individuals. Yet few of these studies have examined the consequences for ongoing social interaction. This experiment was designed to investigate the effects of the intermittent presence of risk on cooperation. Our primary question was whether the opportunity to take at infrequent intervals during cooperation has the same disruptive effect as the opportunity to take anytime. To provide an answer, we allowed cooperating subjects to take only during several short intervals which occurred irregularly throughout a session. At all other times the take light was off and pressing the take button had no effect. Subjects then worked under one of several additional conditions in order to provide answers to two other questions: First, will pairs who cooperate when the opportunities to take are infrequent continue to choose to cooperate when the take opportunities are made more frequent? Second, will pairs who are noncooperative with infrequent opportunities to take begin cooperating if a larger cooperative reward is used?

METHOD

Five pairs of female students were studied from five to seven sessions in the standard setting. The number of sessions for each pair was determined by the stability of the response patterns under the various conditions. The sequence of conditions is shown in Table 5-5.

The procedures through the baseline of Session 2 were similar to the large-risk experiment, except that the initial

Table 5-5

Conditions Defining Intermittent Risk Experiment

Session	Segment	Counts[a] Cooperation (each subject)	Individual	Minutes in segment
1	1 – 4 Training			
2	5 Baseline: co-operation or individual responding	4	3	30
	6 Risk: cooper-ation with taking (VT 30-minute schedule) or individual responding	4	3	90
3	7 Baseline: cooperation or individual responding	4	3	30
	8 Risk: cooper-ation with taking (VT 30-minute schedule) or individual responding	4	3	90

Additional sessions: If cooperation with VT 30-minute schedule, VT 5-minute and continuous-take schedules were used.

If noncooperation with VT 30-minute schedule, cooperative reinforcer was increased to 9 counts.

[a]Each count was worth .1¢.

rewards for cooperation and individual work were 4 and 3 counts, respectively.[3] In the instructions describing the take procedure, subjects were told that the take button would be on "at various times . . . when both switch to work with the other person." During the risk segments in Sessions 2 and 3, the opportunity to take was scheduled intermittently rather than continuously. Three 2-minute periods in which taking was possible were scheduled at irregular (variable) times during the 90-minute segment (VT 30-minute schedule). During the 2-minute periods, the take buttton was operative (indicated by the amber light next to the button) only if both subjects had switched to the cooperative task. At all other times the take button was not operative when subjects switched to cooperation. If subjects were working individually, no signal indicated the occurrence of take periods.

If a pair did not cooperate by the end of Session 3, the reward for cooperation was increased to 9 counts during Session 4 and subsequent sessions. If cooperation eventually resulted under the VT 30-minute schedule (with either the 4-, 5-, or 9-count reward), the frequency of 2-minute take periods was increased to an average of one every 5 minutes (VT 5-minute schedule). Finally, for pairs who cooperated under the VT 5-minute schedule, taking was made possible continuously during the periods of cooperation (as in the previous risk experiments).

RESULTS

Even occasional opportunities to take resulted in at least some disruption in all pairs. For the disrupted pairs an increase in cooperative rewards tended to increase

[3]Two pairs, C–H and J–K, required the 2-count difference in task rewards before cooperating.

cooperation. For the eventually cooperative pairs an increase in the opportunities to take typically eliminated cooperation.

As Table 5-6 shows, none of the pairs were wholly cooperative under the VT 30-minute schedule while receiving 4 or 5 counts for cooperation. With taking possible less than 7% of the time, two pairs cooperated for intermittent periods while three were eventually noncooperative. For the sample as a whole, this intermittent risk schedule explained 87% of the variance in the proportion of cooperative responses (means. baseline .99, risk .18).

Table 5-6

Summary of Effects: Intermittent Risk Experiment
(VT-30 minute: 4 or 5 Counts for Cooperation)

Pattern	n	%
Eventual Noncooperation		
Noncooperation without taking	2	40
Cooperation disrupted by taking	1	20
Mixed Cooperation/Noncooperation		
Alternating periods of cooperation with taking and noncooperation	2	40
Total:	5	100

Figure 5-1 shows the rates of cooperation and individual responding under all of the conditions. Of the three eventually noncooperative pairs under the VT 30-minute schedule with the 4- or 5-count reward for cooperation, two pairs, L–G and L–S, never cooperated or took. The third pair, C–H, cooperated during the first half of Session 2 before one subject took, and then worked individually for the remainder of Session 2 and all of Session 3. The remaining two pairs, T–K and H–L cooperated often

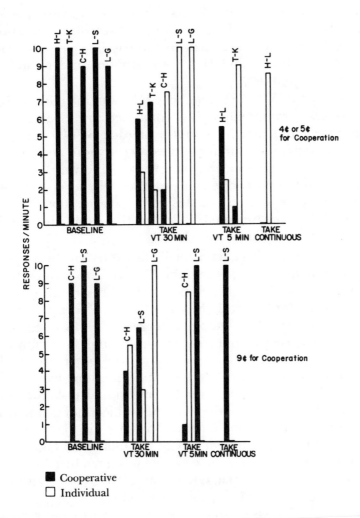

Figure 5-1 Cooperative and individual response rates during total time under the various schedules. The upper half of the figure shows the response rates under the intial 4- or 5-count reward magnitudes for cooperation. The lower half shows the response rates of the three groups who worked under the 9-count reward magnitude for cooperation after little cooperation under the initial magnitudes.

and took whenever possible. As periods of individual work were also interspersed, their overall rates of cooperation were substantially lower than in the baseline periods. Pair T–K worked three, and H–L four, sessions under the VT 30-minute schedule.

When the VT 5-minute schedule was introduced for the two cooperating pairs, T–K continued to cooperate and take during the first 30 minutes of each of two sessions. However, for the remainder of these two sessions and during an entire third session, the pair worked individually. Pair H–L continued to cooperate and take whenever possible during a single session. In this pair's final session, taking was possible continuously. Under this condition both cooperation and taking ceased.

In two of the three pairs totally disrupted by the VT 30-minute schedule, increasing the reward for cooperation from 4 or 5 to 9 counts substantially increased the rate of cooperation. For pair L–S a high rate of cooperation, broken by periods of taking, emerged after two sessions. Pair C–H also cooperated frequently, although both subjects switched repeatedly from one task to the other and took several times during the two sessions. The third pair, L–G, continued to work totally on the individual task for two sessions. One or the other of the subjects occasionally switched to cooperation, but if her partner did likewise, the other would return immediately to the individual task.

When the VT 5-minute schedule was introduced for the two newly cooperating pairs, L–S continued to cooperate and no taking occurred. The pair remained totally cooperative during a final session when taking was possible continuously, and also when the reward was reduced to 4 counts during the last 30 minutes of that session. For pair C–H, however, the VT 5-minute schedule resulted in increased taking and individual responding by the end of the first session. During the second session the pair worked solely on the individual task.

DISCUSSION

Occasional opportunities to take were highly effective in disrupting cooperation. When pairs were largely cooperative under one of the two intermittent take schedules, increasing the opportunities to take generally eliminated cooperation. Even under the largest reward for cooperation, where subjects could each earn over $5 per hour, two of three pairs stopped cooperating when taking could occur frequently (but not continuously).

In the large-risk experiment with taking possible continuously during periods of cooperation, 24 pairs never made any cooperative responses and one made only a single cooperative response. Therefore, subjects were rarely or never rewarded for cooperating when taking was possible. Thus it might be argued that if subjects would only try to cooperate under risk conditions, they might find it more attractive than taking. In the present experiment, however, four pairs ultimately cooperated for substantial periods under the VT 30-minute take schedule (two after the higher reward for cooperation). Yet, in only one pair did cooperation continue when opportunities to take were more frequent or continuous. Thus the results emphasize the dependence of rate of cooperation on the frequency of periods with taking, regardless of the rewards received during intervening periods of cooperation.

Distributing the Ability to Take:
The Asymmetric Risk Experiment

We began our investigation of conditions potentially disruptive of cooperation by focusing on a characteristic of rewards which emerges only in multiperson situations—their *comparative* magnitude. But it is not only rewards that may be distributed differentially in this situation; it is also possible for the amount of risk to be asymmetrically borne. Differences in the distribution of risk are common, and may even be the rule in cooperative settings. For example, only one of two partners may have the ability to embezzle—he handles the books; or only one may understand the technical secrets on which the business is based.

Thus the objective of this experiment was to determine if the risk effect holds when only one subject is exposed to possible loss. His partner, not he, is able to take during cooperation. Since the disruption of cooperation generally follows taking, it might be argued that eliminating one of the two possible takers should substantially increase the number of cooperating pairs. There is simply less chance that taking will occur. On the other hand, the subject who cannot take continues to risk loss of money if he cooperates, and he has no means of retaliation. If taken from, he cannot even try to get his money back. Thus he may be even more prone to avoid cooperation and the attendant risk.

Deutsch and Krauss (1962) compared the effects of symmetric and asymmetric threats in their two-person "trucking game," where either one or both subjects could harm the other. The injurious act was the use of a gate which could be lowered to block the other's more profitable truck route. They found that a cooperative resolution, i.e., subjects alternatively using the more profitable route, was far more common in the asymmetric threat condition.

METHOD

Eight female and eight male pairs were scheduled for four sessions in the standard setting. The sequence of conditions is shown in Table 5-7.

Only Subject A was able to take during risk segments. Subject B's take button was covered but his "take light"

Table 5-7

Conditions Defining Asymmetric Risk Experiment

Session		Segment	Counts[a] Cooperation (each subject)	Individual	Minutes in segment
1	1–4	Training			
2	5	Baseline: co-operation or individual responding	4	3	30
	6	Asymmetric risk: cooperation with taking for Subject A or individual responding	4	3	90
3	7	Baseline	4	3	30
	8	Asymmetric risk	4	3	90
4	9	Baseline	4	3	30
	10	Asymmetric risk	4	3	90

[a]Each count was worth .1¢.

remained operative. A label next to B's take light indicated that when it was on the other person could take $1 of his money. As in the take segments of the large-risk experiment, taking was possible whenever both subjects switched to cooperation.

RESULTS AND DISCUSSION

Fifteen of the 16 pairs completed the baseline sequence. One pair (male) was not studied further after failing to cooperate during the baseline in Session 2.

Once again the effect of risk on cooperation was marked, although not as extreme as in the large-risk experiment. Even with only one subject able to take, the majority of pairs were totally noncooperative throughout the risk condition. As Table 5-8 shows, only four of the 15 pairs (all female) were cooperative at the conclusion of the experiment. For the sample as a whole, asymmetric risk explained 50% of the variance in the proportion of cooperative responses (means: baseline .98, asymmetric risk .34).

Table 5-8

Summary of Effects: Asymmetric Risk Experiment

Pattern	n	%
Eventual cooperation		
Cooperation without taking	2	13
Delayed cooperation without taking	2	13
Eventual noncooperation		
Taking and noncooperation	5	33
Noncooperation without taking	3	20
Cooperation disrupted by taking	2	13
Cooperation disrupted without taking	1	7
Total:	15	99

As with symmetric risk, noncooperation was typically the product of taking, rather than of initial avoidance of risk. Most of the taking occurred in the first take segment, after which the disadvantaged subject generally remained on the individual task.

Perhaps the most important aspect of the study of asymmetric risk is the evidence of an isomorphism between individual and pair behavior. The experiment provides evidence to suggest that the behavior of symmetric pairs may be predicted on the basis of individual probabilities of taking. Let us first assume that the behavior of those subjects who could take in the asymmetric risk situation can be used to determine the likelihood that a given individual from our student population will initiate taking. There were 12 subjects in the asymmetric risk experiment whose partners did not follow a total avoidance strategy and therefore had an opportunity to take. Seven of these 12 subjects took. If we assume that the probability of any individual initiating taking is approximately .58, and that individuals are randomly distributed into pairs, the probability that any pair will contain at least one taker is approximately .83. If we further assume that taking inevitably leads to noncooperation, and that noncooperation rarely occurs without taking (a supposition supported by our original large-risk findings), we would predict that approximately 83% of all pairs would be noncooperative in the symmetric large-risk experiment. This prediction compares well with our earlier findings. In the large-risk extended experiment, 86% of the pairs were noncooperative at the end of four sessions.

PART III: CROSS-PROCEDURAL AND CROSS-POPULATION REPLICATIONS

We have previously noted the importance of replication in establishing the external validity of experimental findings. Following the initial risk experiments, Marwell's previously arranged year in Norway provided us with an opportunity to replicate the risk studies with a sample of Norwegian students. To undertake these experiments, however, it was necessary to design a second, less complex apparatus to be taken to Norway. This, in turn, necessitated changes in procedures. The resultant method was sufficiently different from the original to necessitate a test of the hypothesis that the same striking risk results would still obtain.

In all, three experiments with this apparatus are reported in this chapter. First, the large-risk experiment was replicated with subjects drawn from the original American student population, but using the simplified apparatus and procedures. Second, these results were replicated cross-culturally in Norway. Finally, the same apparatus was also used in the United States to study the behavior of mixed-sex pairs of subjects.

A Cross-Procedural Replication: The Simplified Setting Experiment

Subjects.   Subjects were 20 male and 20 female student volunteers who were paired into 20 like-sex groups. The university in which subjects were recruited and the method of recruitment were identical to those of the original large-risk study.

The Simplified Setting.   Both subjects and the experimenter were seated in a large room but were hidden from each other by partitions. A sketch of the setting is shown in Fig. 5-2. The partitions were arranged so that all could see the display panel and bulletin board in the front of the room. Each subject faced a box 6 by 4 by 5 inches (15.25 by 10 by 12.75 cm) with a response button, a task selection switch, and a take button mounted on it. A buzzer was located in the box. In the front of the room facing both subjects and the experimenter was a large panel with two counters showing each subject's earnings, and lights which indicated each subject's response button presses and switch choices. The display panel was easily visible from the subject's seats. Figure 5-3 presents a schematic display of the panels.

Training Procedure.   Subjects reported to separate waiting areas and were taken separately to the laboratory room

Figure 5-2 Diagram of simplified experimental setting.

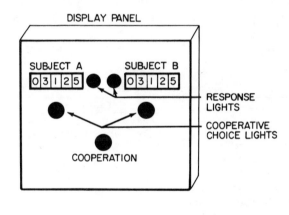

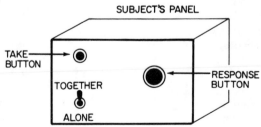

Figure 5-3 Diagram of subject's panel and display panel.

to avoid meeting or identifying their work partners. The sequence of conditions is shown in Table 5-9. Subjects were first instructed on the operation of the individual and cooperative tasks and the task selection switch. The basic response for either the individual or the cooperative task was the press of the task button. Subjects could perform either task only once per trial. A trial was signaled by the experimenter, who rang a small bell. The subjects then had a maximum of 7 seconds within which to make a response. In practice, less than one trial per 1,000 ever resulted in no task performance, and most trials involved task behavior within the first 2 seconds of the trial.

A push of the task button illuminated a white light on the display panel. The light was labeled with the subject's identifying letter (A or B) and remained on as long as the

Table 5-9

Conditions Defining Replication Experiments

| Segment | Counts[a] | | Length of |
	Cooperation (each subject)	Individual	segment (trials)
1 Individual responding	none	1	30
2 Cooperation	1	none	30
3 Baseline: cooperation or individual responding	3	2	10
4 Reversal: cooperation or individual responding	2	3	30
5 Baseline: cooperation or individual responding	3	2	30
6 Risk: cooperation with taking or individual responding	3	2	200
7 Baseline: cooperation or individual responding	3	2	30

[a]Each count was worth 1/3¢ with American subjects; 2 øre (2/7 ¢) with Norwegian subjects.

button was held down. On the individual task the subject
had only to make his light flash. On the cooperative task
the subjects' lights had to be on simultaneously at least
briefly.

Subjects chose between the tasks by operating a toggle
switch. The cooperative task could be performed only if
both subjects chose to work together. If either or both
chose to work alone, only the individual task could be
performed by both subjects. A red light on the front display panel was illuminated whenever a subject switched to
"work with other person" (cooperate). Thus each subject
was always informed of his partner's task choice. When both
subjects chose to cooperate, a green light on the display
panel, labeled "cooperation," also went on. Subjects could
switch tasks at any time—during a trial or between trials.

Following a successful task response, the experimenter
registered the specified number of counts on the labeled
counters on the display panel. Each count was worth one-
third of a cent. The amount subjects could earn per trial
on each task was told to them and also posted in front of
the room on the bulletin board. During the instructions
each subject earned 1 count for every cooperative or individual response. After the instructions and 60 practice
responses (Segments 1 and 2), five trials were included in
which either or both of the subjects were told to switch
from one task to the other, so that the subjects could see
the effects of various combinations of task choices on their
earnings.

Baseline Conditions. Subjects then worked 10 trials
under baseline conditions (Segment 3) to determine
whether cooperation would be maintained by a 1-count
(one-third of a cent) difference in reinforcement. Subjects received 2 counts for working individually and 3
counts for cooperation. No taking was possible, regardless
of task choice.

To demonstrate that the greater earnings were maintaining cooperation under baseline conditions, rewards for the two tasks were then reversed (Segment 4). Individual work received 3 counts and cooperation 2. Thirty trials were included under these conditions. At least 80% of these trials had to be individual task responses for the subjects to continue. All pairs met this criterion.

Finally, subjects worked an additional 30 trials under the original baseline conditions (Segment 5), with 3 counts for cooperation and 2 counts for working alone. When this change was instituted, subjects were instructed that the rewards would not be changed again for the remainder of the experiment. Pairs once again had to evidence at least 80% cooperation to continue. Again all pairs met the criterion.

Risk Conditions. Subjects were then instructed in the use of the take button. This button, while uncovered previously, was not labeled or operative. The subjects were told: "This is the take button. Whenever you press this button you take 300 points (i.e., counts)—$1—from the other person. If he has less than 300 points, you take whatever amount he has." Each subject then pressed the button once, and the transfer of counts was carried out each time (resulting, of course, in the original earned totals being restored).

A press of the take button briefly activated a loud buzzer in the panel of the subject taking. If both subjects pressed the take button nearly simultaneously and the experimenter could not distinguish which subject's buzzer sounded first (they had different tones), a simultaneous take was declared and no transfers effected. This occurred very infrequently.

Subjects were then shown that the take button was available only when cooperation had been selected. Each in turn was instructed to switch to work alone and then try to take from the other person, in order to show that the take buttons now did not work. Takes could be made at any time that the cooperative task was selected by both subjects. Subjects did not have to wait for the beginning of a new trial. If a take did occur, however, a second could not be performed until a new trial was signaled.

The instructions were followed by 200 trials with taking possible (Segment 6). Finally, subjects worked 30 additional trials with risk removed—the original baseline conditions (Segment 7).

Comparison with Methods of Standard Risk Experiment

The major methodological differences between the simplified and standard risk experiments are:

1. Trials. Task performance occurred within trials rather than at an unspecified rate.

2. Task. The cooperative task was much simpler, requiring minimal coordination.

3. Duration of experiment. Whereas the original risk experiment took 4 hours and was split into two sessions, this experiment took less than 2 hours in all. The major difference was the greater training time demanded by the complexity of the standard experimental tasks.

4. Number of task behaviors. As many as 10 task responses per minute were performed under the standard free-operant task conditions—up to 750 task responses under 75 minutes of risk conditions. The use of only 200 trials in this replication, necessitated by the absence of automatic recording and reinforcement equipment, was considered feasible because of the earlier finding that cooperation or noncooperation tended to stabilize quickly

under risk conditions, usually within the first few minutes. It might be noted that time under risk conditions, as opposed to the number of task performance occasions, was reduced only slightly.

5. Rewards per task response. In the previous experiment each task response earned from .2¢ to .3¢ as compared with the .67¢ to 1¢ earned in the present experiment. This change was necessitated by the lower possible rate of performance.

RESULTS

The results replicate those of the original experiment. As Table 5-10 shows, only three of 20 pairs (all male) were eventually cooperative, compared with two of 28 pairs in the original study. Only one of the 17 disrupted pairs showed more than a very brief amount of cooperation, and that ended on trial 80—40% of the risk segment. As in the original study, only the cooperative pairs did not take. For the sample as a whole, risk explained 68% of the variance

Table 5-10

Summary of Effects: Simplified-Risk Setting

Pattern	n	%
Eventual cooperation		
Cooperation without taking	3	15
Eventual noncooperation		
Taking and noncooperation	9	45
Noncooperation without taking	7	35
Cooperation disrupted by taking	1	5
Total:	20	100

in the proportion of cooperative responses (means: baseline .98, risk .15).

Insofar as there was any particular difference between the results of the two studies, it concerned the number of pairs which exhibited what might be called an avoidance pattern—noncooperation with no taking. In the original study every pair which was eventually noncooperative evidenced at least one take. In the present study, seven pairs were noncooperative even though no takes occurred. In six of these pairs one or both of the subjects switched to work alone on the first trial and never changed, thus leaving no opportunity to take.

A Cross-Cultural Replication:
The Basic Norwegian Experiment

METHOD

Subjects were 12 male and 12 female University of Oslo student volunteers who were paired into 12 like-sex pairs.

The simplifed setting and procedure reported in the previous experiment were used, with two necessary exceptions:

1. All instructions were translated into Norwegian, and the experimenter was Norwegian.

2. Rewards for task performance and taking were in Norwegian øre.

The numbers used for the task and taking responses were the same as in the previous experiment. However, 1 count equaled 2 øre. Since 1 øre is approximately one-seventh of a cent, one count was worth approximately two-sevenths of a cent, as opposed to the one-third of a cent in the previous experiment. Similarly, the take was worth approximately $.86 instead of $1.

RESULTS AND DISCUSSION

As Table 5-11 shows, the results full substantiate the dramatic effect of risk on cooperation. Not a single one of the Norwegian pairs was cooperative. In fact, the major difference between the Norwegian and American samples was that the Norwegian sample was almost completely non-cooperative. Only one of the 12 pairs showed any coopera-tive behavior, and that lasted a total of three trials. Less than half of the American pairs were totally noncooperative, although only four had more than 11 cooperative responses. For the Norwegian sample as a whole, risk explained 98% of the variance in the proportion of cooperative responses (means: baseline .98, risk .00).

Table 5-11

Summary of Effects: Cross-Cultural Replication

Pattern	n	%
Eventual noncooperation		
Taking and noncooperation	10	83
Noncooperation without taking	2	17
Total:	12	100

The Norwegian pairs were somewhat more conflictive than the Americans. Although one American pair had over 150 takes, the next greatest number was 14. In one Nor-wegian pair 67 takes occurred, including 31 consecutive trials with simultaneous takes. Another pair had 34 takes. Only two of the Norwegian pairs showed the total avoidance pattern evidenced by 45% of the Americans. In the rest of the Norwegian pairs some taking occurred. Typically, switches to cooperation were followed immediately by a take and a return to the individual task.

Since the findings reported above are substantially the same as those found in the original research, the replications confirm the relationship between interpersonal risk and cooperation while generalizing it beyond the standard setting and the American sample of subjects.

The Effect of Sex Roles: The Mixed-Sex Experiment

In all experiments reported to this point, we followed the time-honored procedure of studying pairs (groups) in which subjects were of one sex. We have seen that there was little systematic difference between the sexes in their propensity to cooperate under large-risk conditions. In this post-sexist world this may be an indication that traditional laboratory segregation is passé—that in recruiting and assigning subjects we should pay little or no attention to sex as a variable. But we were far from sure. We suspected that mixed-sex pairs might behave differently from same-sex pairs, regardless of our previous results.

The pattern of results from previous studies, all using the Prisoner's Dilemma or a modification, has been mixed. Lutzker (1961) found no differences between mixed- and like-sex pairs, while Rapaport and Chammah (1965) found that mixed-sex pairs were less cooperative than male but more cooperative than female pairs. Using a modified Prisoner's Dilemma game (the Maximizing Difference Game) with Belgian students, McNeel, McClintock and Nuttin (1972) found mixed-sex pairs to be significantly more cooperative than like-sex pairs. The cooperativeness of their mixed-sex pairs was due to a decrease in competitiveness on the part of males. Thus, there is at least some evidence that males might be unwilling to take from (exploit) females.

METHOD

Twenty male and 20 female subjects were grouped into 20 mixed-sex pairs. Conditions and all but one of the procedures were identical to those reported for the simplified setting (American subjects). The only new procedure was that the two subjects were simultaneously brought from their separate waiting rooms to the experimental room. No talking was allowed, but in this interval each subject could see that his partner was of the opposite sex.

RESULTS

As Table 5-12 indicates, the effect of risk is once again marked. At the conclusion of the risk condition only six of 20 pairs were cooperative, a proportion only slightly higher than with same-sex pairs. For the sample as a whole, risk explained 52% of the variance in the proportion of cooperative responses (means: baseline .99, risk .33).

Table 5-12

Summary of Effects: Mixed-Sex Experiment

Pattern	n	%
Eventual cooperation		
Cooperation without taking	3	15
Delayed cooperation without taking	2	10
Taking followed by cooperation	1	5
Eventual noncooperation		
Noncooperation without taking	6	30
Taking and noncooperation	8	40
Total:	20	100

Although sex heterogeneity did not significantly affect cooperation, it was not without noticeable effects on behavior. One strikingly different pattern of taking behavior emerged in the mixed-sex pairs. In eight of the nine pairs in which taking occurred, the *first* subject to take was female. Thus it may be that norms against male exploitation of females do insinuate themselves into the laboratory. Alternatively, however, it may be that females are simply more exploitative.

The slightly greater proportion of mixed-sex than same-sex pairs who were cooperative may be attributable to the one new procedure used in the present experiment—the brief visual contact we arranged in order for subjects to identify one another by sex. It could be argued that such contact may affect behavior by "personalizing" one's partner, thus bringing to bear social stimuli which may reduce conflict. Although we will present additional data on this point in Chapter 7, the present results provide preliminary evidence as to the relative unimportance of such brief contact.

CONCLUSION

The eight experiments reported in this chapter all deal with the reliability and generality of the disruptive effects of risk. Together the findings provide strong support for the risk effect. It was fully replicated cross-procedurally and cross-culturally, with mixed-sex as well as same-sex pairs. In addition, neither a major increase in the difference in rewards between cooperation and individual work nor a substantial reduction in the opportunities to take led to cooperation for a majority of pairs. Even when only one of the two subjects could take from the other, most pairs were noncooperative.

In one experiment cooperation was not destroyed by the introduction of risk, but this result further clarifies the basic risk findings. The experiment showed the importance of the consequences of taking in producing disruption. Where taking was not rewarding for the taker, only punishing to the victim, taking did not occur, and cooperation typically was maintained. The possibility that the other would make a profitless response was not a credible threat to cooperation.

CHAPTER 6

ACHIEVING COOPERATION UNDER RISK: PROTECTION AND COMMUNICATION

At least under a range of laboratory conditions, inter-personal risk appears to be an important factor in disrupting cooperation. Let's assume that this relation reflects the impact of risk on cooperation in the world outside the laboratory as well. Given the values stated at the beginning of this book—the desirability of greater cooperation—our next task is clear: to search for those factors which counteract or mitigate the effect. How can we promote cooperation despite the presence of risk?

In Chapters 6, 7, and 8 we look at several possible paths to promoting cooperation. This chapter considers some selected changes in the setting itself: (a) increasing or decreasing the potential for self-protection under conditions of risk; (b) allowing the opportunity for communication between subjects. Both factors are commonly cited as major contributors to mitigating interpersonal difficulties, and may be easily operationalized within the present research design. In all, five experiments are reported, three concerning protection and two involving communication.

Removing the "Safe" Alternative—The Large-Risk, No-Protection Experiment

Several studies of interpersonal bargaining have suggested that the absence of a "safe" alternative to a situation which involves risk tends to force a mutually profitable resolution of the conflict (Kelley, 1965). Applying this interpretation to the present risk setting, we should be able to increase cooperation by eliminating the possibility of avoiding risk by switching to the individual task. Thus in this experiment we made taking possible at any time, regardless of task choice. With this variation, an important change in outcome would result when one subject persisted in taking. Whereas previously his partner could opt for the lower-paying but still profitable individual task, taking could now preempt all other responses, thereby eliminating the possibility of any additional task reward for either subject. It seemed likely that such profitless taking might eventually extinguish and that the more profitable task activity—cooperation—would result.

METHOD

One male and five female pairs were scheduled for six sessions in the sequence of conditions shown in Table 6-1. Pairs worked from two to four sessions during which taking was possible continuously (no protection condition) regardless of task choice. If a high rate of cooperation

Table 6-1

Conditions Defining the No-Protection Experiment

Session		Segment	Counts[a]		Minutes in segment
			Cooperation (each subject)	Individual	
1	1–4	Training			
2–5	5	Baseline: co-operation or individual responding	4	3	30
	6[b]	Risk–no protec-tion: coopera-tion, individual responding, and taking	4	3	90
6		Baseline	4	3	30
		Risk–protection: cooperation with taking or individual responding	4	3	60
		Risk–no protection	4	3	30

[a]Each count was worth .1¢.

[b]If pair cooperated at a high rate during at least 80% of the segment, it was terminated following a session that included the conditions shown in Session 6.

occurred in the no-protection condition, a final session was run which included a segment in which taking was possible only when subjects cooperated (as in the large-risk experiment). This condition was added to determine if cooperation would cease when the safe alternative was introduced.

RESULTS AND DISCUSSION

The absence of an escape from taking resulted in a substantial amount of cooperation, although not without considerable conflict. As Table 6-2 shows, four of the six pairs (three female one male) were eventually cooperative, a proportion significantly greater than under large risk.[1] For the sample as a whole, the no-protection condition explained 19% of the variance in the proportion of cooperative responses (means: baseline .99, no protection .66).

Table 6-2

Summary of Effects: No-Protection Experiment

Pattern	n	%
Eventual cooperation		
Taking followed by cooperation	4[a]	67
Eventual noncooperation		
Taking followed by withdrawal from experiment	2	33
Total:	6	100

[a]One subject withdrew in the final session.

[1]$p < .005$, Fisher Exact Probability test.

The cooperating pairs differed mainly in the time required before cooperation emerged. Cooperation began early in Session 2 for two pairs, in Session 3 for another pair, and in Session 4 for the last pair. Taking occurred in each of these pairs and was nearly continuous prior to cooperation. During this period few task responses of either kind were made. When cooperation began, taking ceased for three of the four pairs. The three continued cooperating during the final session, when taking was possible only during periods of cooperation. The fourth pair began cooperating early in Session 2 and continued thereafter, except for several takes by both subjects at the ends of Sessions 3 and 4. In Session 5, when taking could occur only if subjects cooperated, the subjects began by cooperating. However, following taking by both subjects, one subject had most of his partner's money, and began to work individually. After approximately 30 minutes, the subject who was losing walked out of the experiment and refused to continue.

The remaining two pairs also refused to continue in in the experiment. Although both pairs were originally scheduled for six sessions, one subject in each pair quit following Session 2. In both pairs taking in Session 2 had been continuous. In one of the pairs, the subject who quit had earned slightly more than her partner, while in the other her partner had taken most of the money.

The results thus bear out the importance of a "safe" alternative in the ability of subjects to resolve conflict. However, they also point up the undesirable consequences which can initially result from the extreme conflict— conflict which led three pairs eventually to escape from the experiment itself before they were able to reach a mutually reinforcing settlement.

Counteracting Risk through Warning: The Signaled Avoidance Experiment

Given the general undesirability of conflict, a more promising, and realistically more common, approach to the problem is the creation of conditions through which risks are minimized or avoided. One such means is to increase surveillance over one's resources. In most situations "taking" is not a single-step, momentary occurrence. It requires approach and retreat as well, and provides opportunities for being thwarted by careful opponents. This experiment, then, was designed to investigate the potential of a "warning" for promoting cooperation in the face of risk. A procedure was used in which either subject could avoid the loss of money by immediately switching back to the individual task after the buzzer indicated that a take had been attempted.

METHOD

One male and five female pairs were studied in the sequence of conditions shown in Table 6-3, using the standard setting. Session 2 began with a 30-minute baseline (Segment 5) followed by a 30-minute risk segment (Segment 6). Only pairs who were noncooperative under risk (no more than six of 30 minutes cooperating) proceeded to the avoidance condition (Segment 7). Those who were cooperative under risk worked an additional 60 minutes under the risk conditions to determine if cooperation would continue.

Pairs, noncooperative during risk alone, received the following instructions introducing the avoidance condition:

> Now, if either person switches to work alone within 5 seconds after the "take money" button has been pressed— indicated by the sound of the buzzer—no money will be taken.

Table 6-3

Conditions Defining Signaled Avoidance Experiment

Session		Segment	Counts[a]		Minutes in segment
			Cooperation (each subject)	Individual	
1	1–4	Training			
2	5	Baseline: co-operation or individual responding	4	3	30
	6	Risk: cooper-ation with taking or individual responding	4	3	30
	7[b]	Risk and avoidance: cooperation with taking or individual responding	4	3	60
3	8	Baseline	4	3	30
	9	Risk and avoidance	4	3	90

Additional sessions: Sequence used in Session 3 was repeated in Sessions 4 and 5 or until cooperation developed in the risk-avoidance condition. Then the sequence shown for Session 2 was used for one or two final sessions.

[a]Each count was worth .1¢.
[b]For pairs cooperative in 6, an additional 60 minutes of risk.

The function of the switch was then demonstrated. A 60-minute segment with this signaled take–avoidance procedure followed.

Sessions 3 through 6 (where required) each began with a 30-minute baseline segment. For pairs who did not cooperate during the take–avoidance phase of the previous session, a 90-minute take–avoidance period followed the baseline segment. This sequence was repeated for four sessions, or until cooperation began in the take–avoidance segment. If cooperation began during a take–avoidance segment, the pair's next session included a sequence designed to investigate the reversibility of the take–avoidance effect. The 30-minute baseline was followed by a 30-minute take segment and then a 60-minute take–avoidance segment. Pairs were terminated after one or two of these sessions.

RESULTS

As expected, the opportunity to take without the avoidance condition in Session 2 disrupted cooperation. Five of the six pairs were almost totally noncooperative, with taking occurring in all but one of the pairs.

For the five noncooperative pairs (four female, one male), the take–avoidance condition was highly effective in producing cooperation under risk. As Table 6-4 shows, all five pairs eventually cooperated when take attempts could be thwarted, a proportion significantly higher than under

Table 6-4

Summary of Effects: Signaled Avoidance Experiment

Pattern (during risk avoidance)	n	%
Eventual cooperation		
Delayed cooperation without taking	3	80
Taking followed by cooperation	2	20
Total:	5[a]	100

[a]Excludes pair cooperative with risk alone.

large risk.[2] For these five pairs, risk with take–avoidance explained only 2% of the variance in the proportion of cooperative responses (means: baseline .99, take–avoidance .99).

Figure 6-1 shows the cooperative and individual response rates for the five noncooperative pairs during the total time under baseline, taking (risk), and take–avoidance conditions (four to six sessions). The delay which preceded cooperation in the take–avoidance condition is reflected in cooperative response rates which are lower than those under baseline conditions. Cooperation began in Session 2 for pairs G–M and D–T and in Session 4 for pairs M–B,

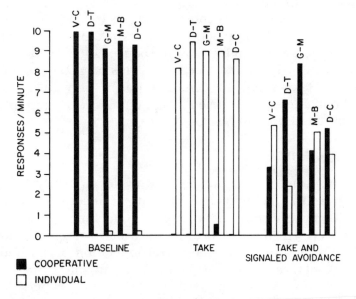

Figure 6-1 Cooperative and individual response rates during baseline, take, and take-signaled avoidance conditions.

[2]$p < .005$, Fisher Exact Probability test.

D–C, and V–T. All pairs ceased cooperating when the possibility of avoidance was removed (with taking still possible), but began cooperating again when avoidance was reinstated.

Taking was attempted in every take–avoidance segment. The number of take attempts was usually less than 20, with a range from 1 to 155. In four of the five initially noncooperative pairs, the number of attempted takes per segment decreased following cooperation. Only four attempts were successful—three by the same subject in pair M–B and one in pair V–C. The remainder were nullified by switches to the individual task—all but five by the subject being taken from.

The sixth pair (not shown in Fig. 6-1) cooperated from the outset. Although both subjects took once soon after the possibility of taking was introduced, they cooperated immediately thereafter. Because of this persistent cooperation, the take–avoidance condition was not introduced. The pair remained cooperative throughout Session 2 and under similar conditions in Session 3.

DISCUSSION

Over time the opportunity to avoid monetary loss by switching to the individual task after an attempted take was highly effective in producing cooperation. However, there were large differences between pairs—approximately 180 minutes—in the time before cooperation began under take–avoidance. Once cooperation began, all pairs were generally successful in avoiding takes and experienced little disruption in cooperation. The absence of many successful takes contrasts with the substantial number of take attempts even after the emergence of cooperation. The fact that take attempts entailed little risk and minimal disruption may have been responsible for their persistence.

Creating Nonrisk Conditions: The Free-Operant Avoidance Experiment

With the signaled avoidance procedure, subjects had no difficulty nullifying almost every take. Their capacity for perfect surveillance and the opportunity to make nullifying responses provided them with virtual security from the potential risk. In practice then, the risk was more apparent than real, and subjects eventually adapted to the realities by cooperating. A more common avoidance procedure, however, is the performance of some kind of anticipatory response in order to render the attempt to take impossible, or at least make it very difficult. In order to protect valuable resources, locks are installed, money is placed in safes, guards are provided. Such procedures often require considerable effort and usually entail some cost.

This experiment considers one version of such anticipatory avoidance. A free-operant response was made available to the subjects with which either of them could prevent *all* taking. If either subject made this response, neither he nor his partner could take. The response prevented taking for only a short, specified period of time, and had to be repeated periodically to reinstate conditions in which taking was not possible. Time intervals of several lengths were studied to determine the shortest one under which cooperation would be maintained. In comparison with the signaled avoidance procedure, free-operant avoidance required a much larger number of responses and continuous monitoring in order to avoid takes. Thus, we expected this procedure to be less effective in promoting cooperation.

For pairs who cooperated in the avoidance condition, a small cost for each avoidance response was introduced to determine whether that response would be suppressed and taking less effectively avoided. Some research in nonsocial settings (Weiner, 1963) has found that a "response cost" leads to substantially reduced rates of response.

METHOD

Five female and two male pairs were studied in the sequence of conditions shown in Table 6-5. The standard setting was modified to include a second (avoidance) but-

Table 6-5

Conditions Defining Free-Operant Avoidance Experiment

Session		Segment	Counts[a]		Minutes in segment
			Cooperation (each subject)	Individual	
1	1–4	Training			
2	5	Baseline: cooperation or individual responding	4	3	30
	6	Risk: cooperation with taking or individual responding	5	3	30
	7[b]	Risk and avoidance: cooperation with taking and 30-second avoidance or individual responding	5	3	60

Additional sessions: Same sequence as in Session 2. If cooperation with avoidance, interval was reduced to 10 seconds. If noncooperation, interval was lengthened to 180 seconds. A 1-count cost for each avoidance response was introduced following avoidance responding and cooperation.

[a]Each count was worth .1¢.
[b]For pairs cooperative in 6, an additional 60 minutes of taking.

ton and light on the panel; these were located above the take button and light. A press of the avoidance button by either subject turned off the take button and light for a specified period of time (indicated on a label next to the button). The light next to the avoidance button went on for the duration of that interval, regardless of task choice.

As in the previous avoidance experiment the baseline in Session 2 was followed by a 30-minute risk segment with taking possible. Because of the cost-avoidance treatment which was to be introduced later, the reward for coopera-tion during the risk segment and all subsequent risk and take–avoidance segments was raised from 4 counts to 5 counts. Thus, when the 1-count cost for each avoidance response was introduced, cooperation would remain more profitable than individual responding even if a substantial number of avoidance responses were made. Subsequent procedures differed, depending upon whether pairs were cooperative or uncooperative in the 30-minute take seg-ment.

Noncooperative Pairs. For pairs who were noncoopera-tive in the 30-minute take segment in Session 2, the avoid-ance button on each panel was uncovered and demonstrated. Subjects received the following instructions:

> *Each of you now has a button which you can press to turn off the "take money" button for 30 seconds, even though both of you have switched to work with the other person. Pressing the top button once will turn off the take money button for 30 seconds. Pressing the top button again while the take money button is still off will restart the 30-second period.*

A 60-minute period with both the 30-second free-operant avoidance schedule and taking in effect concluded the session. Each subsequent session included a 30-minute baseline, 30-minute take segment, and a 60-minute take–avoidance segment. If high rates of cooperation failed to develop after two sessions with the 30-second interval, it was lengthened to 180 seconds. If cooperation developed with the 30-second interval, it was reduced to 10 seconds. If a pair began cooperating during any of the take-only segments, and continued to cooperate in the following take–avoidance segment, it was not studied further.

When the shortest of the avoidance intervals that produced cooperation was determined, a 1-count cost for each avoidance response was introduced. In addition to preventing taking, each press of the avoidance button substracted 1 count from the subject's own counter. The size of the cost was shown on a label next to the avoidance button. If the response cost eliminated avoidance responding and cooperation, the avoidance intervals were lengthened to either 30 seconds, 180 seconds, or 600 seconds until avoidance responding and cooperation reoccurred.

Cooperative Pairs. For pairs who were cooperative in the 30-minute take segment in Session 2, take conditions were continued for the remainder of the session. In Session 3 the 30-minute take segment was followed by the introduction of the 30-second avoidance interval to determine if avoidance responses would also be made by previously cooperative subjects.

RESULTS

The opportunity to take in Session 2 disrupted cooperation in five of the seven pairs. Taking occurred in three of the noncooperative pairs.

For the two pairs who cooperated without taking throughout Session 2, the 30-second avoidance condition was introduced in Session 3 following the baseline and 30-minute take segment. Neither pair developed a stable pattern of avoidance responding.

For the noncooperative pairs, the avoidance condition

was eventually highly effective in producing cooperation under risk. As Table 6-6 shows, all five pairs (four female, one male) cooperated totally in one of the no-cost avoidance conditions, a proportion significantly greater than under large risk.[3] There was no difference in proportion of cooperative responses to be explained by risk with avoidance (means in both the baseline and avoidance conditions were 1.00).

Table 6-6

Summary of Effects: Free-Operant Avoidance (No-Cost) Experiment

Pattern (during risk avoidance)	n	%
Eventual cooperation		
Delayed cooperation without taking		
180-second interval	1	20
30-second interval	1[a]	20
30-second and 10-second intervals	2	40
Delayed cooperation with taking		
30-second and 10-second intervals	1	20
Total:	5[b]	100

[a] Eventually cooperated in take-only segment.
[b] Excludes pairs cooperative with risk alone.

Figure 6-2 shows the mean cooperative and individual response rates for the five noncooperative pairs during the total time under the baseline, take (risk), and take-avoidance conditions (six to eight sessions). Four of the five pairs began cooperating at a high rate in the 30-second avoidance condition and the fifth cooperated when the avoidance interval was increased to 180 seconds. One of the four pairs cooperating in the 30-second avoidance

[3] $p < .005$, Fisher Exact Probability test.

condition continued to cooperate in the take segment preceding the 10-second condition and was not studied
further. The remaining three pairs were studied with the
interval reduced to 10 seconds. All three continued to cooperate. For these pairs cooperation *never* occurred during
the take segments without avoidance.

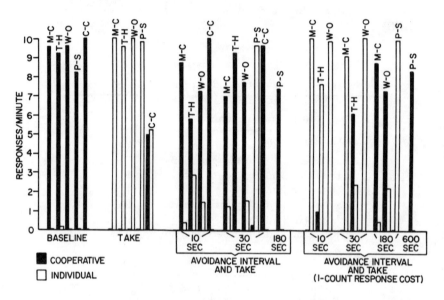

Figure 6-2 Cooperative and individual response rates during
baseline, take, and take-free-operant avoidance conditions.

Overall, a single take occurred in the 30-second avoidance condition, and nine takes occurred in the 10-second
avoidance condition—all in pair T–J. Avoidance response
rates during cooperation (shown in Table 6-7) ranged from
approximately four to 35 per minute.

For the four pairs making avoidance responses and
cooperating, the 1-count cost for each response was introduced. The avoidance interval for each pair was the final
one used in the previous no-cost segment—180 seconds for

Table 6-7

Avoidance Responses per Minute for Initially Noncooperative Pairs

	Avoidance Interval						
	(No cost)			(1-count response cost)			
	10 seconds	30 seconds	180 seconds	10 seconds	30 seconds	180 seconds	600 seconds
M-C	12.8[a] (1)	10.1[a] (2)		0 (1)	.1 (1)	.7[a] (1)	
T-H	34.5[a] (3)	7.5[a] (1)		2.3 (1)	2.6[a] (1)		
W-O	23.3[a] (2)	11.4[a] (2)		.2 (2)	0 (1)	1.7[a] (1)	
P-S		1.0 (2)	8.0[a] (1)			0 (2)	
C-C		3.6[a] (1)					.1[a] (1)

[a]Substantial cooperation (i.e., five or more cooperative responses per minute).

P–S and 10 seconds for M–C, T–H, and W–O. The addition of the response cost eliminated almost all avoidance responding and cooperation for all four pairs. However, when the avoidance interval was lengthened, both avoidance responding and cooperation eventually increased.

DISCUSSION

The free-operant avoidance procedure was as effective as signaled avoidance in producing high rates of cooperation with the opportunity to take. With the exception of one pair, almost all taking was avoided by the high rates of avoidance responding. Over time, most subjects apparently found that the aversive consequences of taking outweighted the reinforcing ones which led to the taking initially.

A small added cost for avoidance responding was effective in almost totally eliminating the avoidance behavior. The magnitude of the suppression was unexpected, since even frequent avoidance responses costing 1 count would have continued to make a high rate of cooperation profitable. Each subject's avoidance response rate would have had to exceed 20 per minute (a rate well above the six per minute needed to keep the take button inoperative under the 10-second interval) before cooperation would have become less profitable than working individually. In fact, if each pair's avoidance response rates in the last no-cost segment had continued when the response cost was introduced, three of the four pairs would have continued to profit by cooperating.

The finding that subjects will readily take advantage of avoidance procedures in cooperative situations with risk has not been apparent in studies using mixed-motive matrix games such as the Prisoner's Dilemma. There, subject intent is unclear in that avoidance and exploitative responses are confounded. The only way in which a subject

can avoid the lowest outcome is to make an exploitative
choice. However, if even small costs will retard or prevent
effective avoidance, the practical application of these procedures may be more limited than the simple economics
of a situation might suggest.

Preventing Conflict through Talking:
The Open Communication Experiment

"Keep them talking instead of fighting." "The problem
is really one of a breakdown in communication." Explanations and suggestions such as these for conflict and its
reduction are probably the most common of any to be found
in both the professional and popular literature. It is widely
argued that opening channels of communication is the key
to stopping wars, parent–child hostilities, and conflicts of
all types. Thus it is to the following question in our original
setting that this experiment and the next one turn: Can
communication promote cooperation where only conflict
and avoidance exist?

Communication in the risk setting could serve various
ends. Cooperation, for example, might be facilitated by
promises, information exchange, or even threats, while
individual gain might be furthered by broken agreements
and deceit. The results of previous studies in different
settings are inconsistent regarding the effects of communication in situations with risk. While studies of matrix
games have generally found that any form of communication substantially increases cooperation (Scodel, Minas,
Ratoosh, & Lipetz, 1959; Radlow & Weidner, 1966;
Bixenstine, Levitt, & Wilson, 1966; Pillsuk, Winter,
Chapman, & Hass, 1967; Swennson, 1967; Wichman, 1970;
Voissem & Sistrunk, 1971; Swingle & Santi, 1972), studies of
bargaining have found the effects to be more limited. In
Deutsch and Krauss' "trucking game" research (Krauss and

Deutsch, 1966), resolution of conflict was greatest when communication was compulsory, at the point of deadlock, and under conditions of unilateral rather than bilateral threat.

This experiment and the next were designed to investigate the effects of the ability to communicate on the relation between large risk and cooperation. The conditions in this first experiment were intended to maximize the effects of communication in facilitating cooperation. Therefore, subjects were permitted to talk freely during all periods of large risk.

METHOD

Six male and six female pairs were studied for three sessions in the standard setting. The sequence of conditions is shown in Table 6-8.[4] Following the demonstration of large risk prior to Segment 6, microphones were placed in each subject's room and tested to show that they were operative. The microphones were available during 60-minute risk segments in Sessions 2 and 3. In addition, a 15-minute risk segment without communication was included at the end of each of the two risk sessions to determine whether accommodations reached through agreement or other verbal interchange would be maintained when the possibility of communication was removed. The experimenter monitored and tape recorded all conversations. The microphones were removed from the rooms whenever communication was not available.

RESULTS

The ability to communicate very substantially reduced the disruptive effects of risk on cooperation. Nine of 12

[4]One pair required the 2-count difference in task rewards before cooperating.

Table 6-8

Conditions Defining Communication Experiment

Session	Segment	Counts[a] Cooperation (each subject)	Individual	Minutes in segment
1	1–4	Training		
2	5	Baseline: cooperation or individual responding	3	3	30
	6	Risk and communication: cooperation with taking or individual responding	3	2	60
	7	Risk: cooperation with taking or individual responding	3	2	15
3	8	Baseline	3	2	30
	9	Risk and communication	3	2	60
	10	Risk	3	2	15

[a]Each count was worth .1¢.

pairs (six female, three male) were cooperative at the conclusion of the risk condition, a proportion significantly greater than under large risk.[5] Another pair (male) was cooperative throughout most of the condition. All but two of these 10 pairs began cooperating within 15 minutes of the onset of the opportunity to communicate. The removal of communication during the last 15 minutes of each session had no effect on the cooperative behavior of any pair. For the sample as a whole, risk and communication explained only 13% of the variance in the proportion of co-

[5]$p < .005$, x^2 test.

operative responses (means: baseline .99, risk and communication .77).

As Table 6-9 shows, the most common pattern of response entailed far less disruption than was characteristic in the large-risk experiment. Six pairs eventually cooperated without taking. In five of these, cooperation resumed almost immediately following the onset of large-risk conditions, while a sixth pair began to cooperate early in Session 3. One other pair also cooperated very quickly without taking, but ceased cooperating on three occasions for periods ranging from 5 to 10 minutes during the latter part of Session 3.

In all of these pairs, cooperation was immediately preceded by a straightforward verbal agreement to cooperate. The following are examples of the kinds of agreements reached:

> *What we have here is a problem of mutual trust.*
> *Right, Okay. I won't push it if you won't push it.*
> *Ah, yeah. All right, I will go along with that.*

Table 6-9

Summary of Effects: Communication Experiment

Pattern	n	%
Eventual cooperation		
Cooperation without taking	6	50
Taking followed by cooperation	3	25
Eventual noncooperation		
Taking and noncooperation	2	17
Mixed cooperation/noncooperation		
Periods of cooperation without taking and noncooperation	1	8
Total:	12	100

In another case:

> *Listen, if I put mine (switch) on working with you and we*
> *don't do it, (press the take button) we can make twice as*
> *much, right?*
> *Right, okay.*
> *Yeah. Then I can push the button?*
> *Well, I wouldn't do it to you.*
> *Okay, we won't do it.*
> *Okay.*

All but one cooperating pair followed their agreements with conversation on other topics in both communication segments.

Less common in this experiment was taking and delayed cooperation. The three pairs which fit this pattern each had a similar history of a broken agreement which was subsequently remade and kept. The behavior of one pair is illustrative. The subjects at first quickly agreed to work together without taking, but immediately broke the agreement. Each subject took once but then made the following agreement, which was subsequently honored.

> *If I have . . . . If I don't . . . . Yeah, let's just say we quit that:*
> *Okay. It's just wasting time, if we don't get along on this*
> *thing instead of doing it before . . . . Right?*
> *Right. Okay.*

A high rate of cooperation without further taking (and accompanied by task-irrelevant conversation) occupied the remaining time with communication. In both of the other pairs, the initial agreement was made early in Session 2. A new agreement was made immediately in one but not until Session 3 in the other.

Only two pairs experienced taking and noncooperation —the pattern that was dominant under large-risk conditions without communication. In one of these pairs, subjects made an early agreement that was immediately broken. The victimized subject then rebuffed the suggestions of his partner:

> *Why don't we just work together and forget the yellow button?*
> *No, I don't trust you, A.*

In the other pair one of the subjects took four times. An agreement was discussed but none was made:

> *How about a peace treaty?*
> *Nah.*
> *You want to work with me if I promise not to push the button?*
> *Nah.*
> *Why?*
> *Oh, I don't know.*
> *I've very high standards about . . . cheating. Really. If you want to work, just say so. Work together.*
> *Nah, I probably won't.*
>
> . . . .
>
> *This seems ridiculous.*
> *Yeah, I guess so.*
> *I promise you I won't push the button if you want to . . .*
> *Nah.*

The overall frequency of taking when communication was available was markedly less than in the large-risk experiment without communication.[6] The largest number of pairs had no takes at all, and taking almost completely disappeared after the first 15 minutes of the initial risk segment. Also, in contrast to the large-risk condition, differences in amount taken were small. The difference was more than $1 in only one pair and over $.25 in only one other. The median difference in Session 2 was $.12.

---

[6]For Session 2 the difference was significant, $p < .001$, Mann–Whitney U Test.

In summary, the results strongly support previous studies showing the facilitating effects of communication for cooperation, and in particular show the importance of opportunities that permit rules or agreements to emerge. The results provide only slight evidence of reticence to communicate or the use of communication for threats or deception.

Ending Conflict Through Talking: The Delayed Communication Experiment

In the previous experiment with risk and communication, agreements regarding taking prevented conflict and thus promoted the maintenance of cooperation. This experiment was designed to examine the consequences of communication for behavior once conflict and noncooperation had already been established. Is communication as effective in reestablishing cooperation as it is in preventing conflict? To answer this question, the opportunity to communicate was introduced, following 30 minutes under large-risk conditions without communication.

METHOD

Five male and five female pairs were studied for three sessions in the sequence of conditions shown in Table 6-10.[7] The microphones were placed in the subject's room following the 30-minute risk segment in Session 2.

RESULTS

The disruption of cooperation by risk during the 30-minute risk segment without communication was similar

[7]One pair required the 2-count difference in task rewards before cooperating.

Table 6-10

Conditions Defining Delayed Communication Experiment

| | | Counts[a] | | |
| | | Cooperation (each subject) | Individual | Minutes in segment |
Session	Segment			
1	1–4	Training		
2	5	Baseline: cooperation or individual responding	3	2	30
	6	Risk: cooperation with taking or individual responding	3	2	30
	7	Risk and communication: cooperation with taking or individual responding	3	2	30
	8	Risk: cooperation with taking or individual responding	3	2	15
3	9	Baseline	3	2	30
	10	Risk and communication	3	2	60
	11	Risk	3	2	15

[a]Each count was worth .1¢.

to that found in the original large-risk experiment. Only one pair was cooperative at the end of the segment.

The prior risk period substantially reduced the effects of communication in facilitating cooperation. The introduction of communication led to cooperation in only five of nine previously noncooperative pairs (three female, two male) a proportion less than in the previous experiment but significantly greater than under large risk alone.[8] As

[8]$p < .005$, Fisher Exact Probability test.

in the previous experiment, the removal of communication during the last 15 minutes of each session had no effect on cooperative behavior. For the sample as a whole, risk and communication explained 36% of the variance in the proportion of cooperative responses (means: baseline .97, risk and communication .44).

Table 6-11 shows the effects of communication on the behavior of the nine pairs who were noncooperative following the risk-only segment. In contrast to the infrequent disruption in the previous experiment, the most common response during communication here involved some taking followed eventually by cooperation. An agreement preceded cooperation in three of these four pairs. One other pair was also eventually cooperative, following agreement, but no taking occurred. Of the four noncooperative pairs, two engaged in some taking. Subjects in all four pairs communicated but made no agreements.

Combining both communication experiments, all but one of the pairs which had the opportunity to communicate and eventually cooperated did so after a specific verbal

Table 6-11

Summary of Effects: Delayed Communication Experiment

Pattern (during communication)	n	%
Eventual cooperation		
Taking followed by cooperation	4	44
Delayed cooperation without taking	1	11
Eventual noncooperation		
Taking and noncooperation	2	22
Noncooperation without taking	2	22
Total:	9[a]	99

[a]Excludes pair cooperative with risk alone.

agreement. All subjects, both cooperating and noncooperating, spoke to one another at least briefly.

CONCLUSION

In five experiments we have seen how cooperation increases in the face of risk when (a) a safe alternative to risk is removed; (b) take attempts can be negated or avoided; or (c) subjects can freely communicate. Beyond this similarity, however, the conditions produced important differences in patterns of behavior. First, there were large differences in the time required before cooperation emerged. Subjects tended to cooperate quickly only when they could communicate at the time that risk was introduced. In all other conditions the time that elapsed before cooperation emerged varied considerably, ranging from a few seconds to several hours. Second, there were important differences in the behavior which preceded cooperation. Notable in this regard was the continuous conflict found in the "no-protection" condition. In other conditions subjects worked mainly on the individual task with little or no disruption. A final difference was the persistence of cooperation when the conditions producing it were removed. The cooperation produced by the avoidance procedures typically did not continue when the conditions were removed, while cooperation did continue following removal of the communication or the no-protection conditions. Although the evidence at hand does not allow us to establish the reasons for this difference, comparison of the conditions suggests at least one potentially important factor—the presence or absence of consequences which affect the taking responses themselves. For example, communication led to agreements not to take, thus bringing extralaboratory stimuli to bear on taking behavior. Similarly, where subjects could take while working on either task, cooperation was preceded by a period of bilateral, profitless taking with few task responses made. In this condition taking itself appeared to extinguish. By contrast, takes in both of the present avoidance procedures were either nullified or avoided through relatively effortless responses and little if any money was lost either through taking or missed task responses.

CHAPTER 7

ACHIEVING COOPERATION UNDER RISK: RELATIONS BETWEEN PEOPLE

The "unreality" of the laboratory is not limited to its sterile walls, restricted opportunities for behavior, and personnel in white coats with godlike powers over rewards and punishments. It resides as well in the absence of past histories in relations between people. Subjects were asked to cooperate with partners they have never seen before—or even during—the period in which the experiment occurred. They had never conversed. They knew little of

139

each other's characters. They had established no debts. In short they were operating in a social vacuum.

But cooperation in the real world is most common among those with long-standing relationships. Even with enterprises involving newly acquainted partners, a period of feeling-out and getting-to-know almost inevitably precedes agreement on the enterprise, or getting down to business. The reasons for this seems clear, based on the results to this point. In the absence of structural constraints which can lessen or abridge risk, sources of control beyond the immediate setting itself need to be tapped. These can include newly generated sources of attraction, pacts, sanctions, or cues from past experience which suggest that cooperation is likely. Factors such as these, which are elements of what we term trust, seem to cement many relationships.

This chapter describes experiments designed to examine the effects that different aspects of the relationships between partners have on the likelihood of cooperating under risk. In the first five experiments, the relations studied varied from quite minimal—in which subjects saw each other before the experiment—to maximal—the subjects were married. The next two experiments concerned the effects of making norms and group memberships salient to the subjects. Finally, one experiment concerned an aspect of rewards that may define the nature of a relationship. It involved the reintroduction of the variable with which we began this research—inequity. But this time, inequity was studied in the context of interpersonal risk.

PART I: MINIMAL RELATIONS

Our previous studies, in which we permitted subjects to communicate, clearly showed that under certain circumstances contact can greatly facilitate the emergence of co-operation under risk. With the opportunity to communicate, we witnessed the formation of agreements to cooperate which were upheld even when communication was no longer possible, suggesting that indeed some minimal norm-bound relationship had been established.

However, the nature of this relationship does not become clear until we have also observed the effects of contact prior to the conflict. For example, it is possible that communication is most important not because it permits agreements but simply because it personalizes one's opponent. No longer is he/she a disembodied set of lights and buzzers. Anonymity is banished. One is brought face to face with the humanity of one's opponent, perhaps evoking other social behaviors. Maybe this is the important difference between communication and noncommunication conditions. The "agreements" are just the process through which the underlying effect is realized.

The three experiments presented below grew out of this interpretation of the effects of social relations on co-operation and taking under risk. We began in the first experiment by allowing subjects to see each other briefly prior to the beginning of the experiment. In the second experiment, subjects talked to each other briefly before beginning. In the third experiment subjects were allowed to see each other during the whole of the experiment. All three experiments were conducted using the simplified setting and the sequence of conditions used in the large-risk replication.

The Other Person Is Real: The Pre-Session Visibility Experiment

We began with a very brief personalizing encounter. Subjects were only allowed to see each other before they entered the experimental room itself. We simply called both subjects from their respective waiting rooms at the same time and took them together into the experimental room, where they then each sat behind the screen. Thus this experiment was identical to the mixed-sex experiment reported in Chapter 5, except that same sex pairs were now used. Five male and five female pairs were studied.

RESULTS

Pairs were no more likely to cooperate under a pre-session visibility treatment than in a completely anonymous condition in the simplified setting. As Table 7-1 shows, only one pair (female) eventually cooperated. For the sample as a whole, risk explained 82% of the variance in the proportion of cooperative responses (means: baseline .98, risk .10).

Table 7-1

Summary of Effects: Minimal Relations Experiments

Pattern	Pre-session visibility		Pre-session communication		Visibility	
	n	%	n	%	n	%
Eventual cooperation						
Cooperation without taking	1	10			1	5
Delayed cooperation without taking			3	15	2	10
Taking followed by cooperation			1	5	1	5
Eventual noncooperation						
Noncooperation without taking	6	60	3	15	5	25
Taking and noncooperation	3	30	13	65	11	55
Total	10	100	20	100	20	100

Increasing the Contact: The Pre-Session Communication Experiment

Perhaps just seeing the other person was not enough to personalize him. There was no shared experience. The other person could have been a confederate of the experimenter. Thus we decided to increase the level of interaction prior to the experiment. Subjects were instructed to report to the same waiting room, where they were left together for a minimum of 10 minutes before being brought to the experimental room. When the second subject arrived, he was introduced to the first by name and both were told that they would be together in the experiment. No attempt was made to restrict communication prior to the experiment itself. Ten male and 10 female pairs were studied.

RESULTS

Again, there was practically no difference between this set of subjects and those who did not meet prior to the experimental session. As Table 7-1 shows, four of the 20 pairs (three male, one female) eventually cooperated, almost the same proportion as in the original anonymous treatment. For the sample as a whole, risk explained 65% of the variance in the proportion of cooperative responses (means: baseline .97, risk .20).

Still More Exposure: The Visibility Experiment

Having failed to support the effect of relatively brief "personalizing" encounters, we decided to increase contact further and permit subjects to see one another throughout the experiment. Previous evidence regarding the importance of visibility has been mixed. Wichman (1970) found

that visibility produced greater cooperation in the Prisoner's Dilemma, while McNeel, McClintock, and Nuttin
(1972), using a modification of the Prisoner's Dilemma
(Maximizing Difference Game), found no effect. In
Lindsley's (1966) studies of cooperation, visibility facilitated cooperation between siblings and hindered it between
strangers.

Ten male and 10 female pairs were studied under a
full visibility treatment. Although the subjects did not meet
prior to being seated in the experimental room, the room
itself had no screens hiding them from each other. The subjects were instructed not to talk to each other, but they
could at all times see each other.

RESULTS

Again, there were only slight differences in response
from the basic anonymous treatment. As Table 7-1 shows,
only four of the 20 pairs (three female, one male) eventually
cooperated. For the sample as a whole, risk explained 66%
of the variance in the proportion of cooperative responses
(means: baseline .99, risk .20).

PART II: MAXIMAL RELATIONS

Simply letting people see each other, or talk to each
other for a few minutes, offers at best the possibility of
establishing a very minimal relationship, one that bears
little resemblance to the long-term associations outside the
laboratory. Hence, we decided next to study the effects of
two of the most common long-standing relations.

Common Resources: The Married Couples Experiment

We began by studying married couples—persons whom
we thought would be most likely to cooperate. The conjugal

family is our only widespread "commune." Almost all families have in some degree joint economies, where inputs by one member may be drawn upon by others. Under such conditions it would be economically irrational for a married couple to cease cooperation under the basic conditions of our experiment. By doing so they would decrease their total rewards, and for no apparent reason. At the same time, they could "take" from each other at will—even playfully—as these takes would mean little loss. Whether married couples take or not should thus depend on considerations other than monetary ones: Do they consider taking a "real" enough representative of trust violation to threaten their relationships, or can they treat it as a game and a chance to "play" competitively with each other at no cost?

A total of seven couples were studied, using the simplified setting and risk sequence. In each couple at least one member was a student.

RESULTS

Two of the couples were not studied further because they would not switch to the individual task when appropriate during the baseline segment. Both of these couples reported that not cooperating would "violate the marriage ethic" (in the words of one subject), or would otherwise be contrary to their view of marriage. In this sense they illustrate the extreme cooperativeness of those with close relations. One additional couple cooperated on fewer than half of the trials during the first baseline segment and was not studied further.

As shown in Table 7-2, the remaining four couples were all eventually cooperative, a proportion significantly greater than in original replication with strangers.[1] One of the

---

[1] $p < .005$, Fisher Exact Probability test.

Table 7-2

Summary of Effects: Maximal Relations Experiments

	Married		Friends	
Pattern	*n*	%	*n*	%
Eventual cooperation				
Cooperation without taking	3	75	4	20
Delayed cooperation without taking			5	25
Taking followed by cooperation	1	25	4	20
Eventual noncooperation				
Noncooperation without taking			1	5
Taking and noncooperation			6	30
Total:	4	100	20	100

couples worked on the individual task and took during the first part of the segment. The other three couples neither took nor worked individually on more than five trials. For these four couples there was no difference in proportion of cooperative responses to be explained by risk at the end of the condition (means in both baseline and risk conditions were 1.00). As expected, all couples reported in post-experimental questioning that they would pool their earnings, as they commonly do with any money they have.

Close Past Relationships but Separate Economies: The Best Friends Experiment

To separate the effects of established, presumably trust-provoking past relationships from that of a joint economy, we selected a sample of "best friends" for study. Under guise of a separate investigation, several large introductory classes filled out questionnaires regarding their social lives and identified their best friend on campus. They were also asked to describe their relationships with their best friend in terms of the following scale:

    a. extremely close and very friendly
    b. close and friendly
    c. not particularly close, but friendly
    d. close, but not particularly friendly
    e. not particularly close or friendly

Only those who answered "extremely close and very friendly" were recruited for the experiment. As further evidence of the closeness of the relationships, they were asked to get the specific person they had mentioned to also participate in the experiment. They reported to the experiment together.

Ten female and 10 male pairs were studied, using the simplified setting and risk sequence.

RESULTS

As shown in Table 7-2, friends were much more likely to cooperate than strangers. Thirteen of the 20 best-friend pairs (nine female, four male) were eventually cooperative, a proportion significantly greater than in the original replication with strangers.[2] For the sample as a whole, risk explained 18% of the variance in the proportion of cooperative responses (means: baseline .98, risk .68).

Subjects who had been recruited on the basis of being named as best friends were also asked to indicate their feelings concerning their partners on a postexperimental questionnaire. Only 11 of the 20 rated their relationship with partner as "extremely close and very friendly." The

[2]$p < .005$, x^2 test.

remainder rated the relationship "close and friendly." However, this rating proved unrelated to the emergence of cooperation.

CONCLUSION

The conclusion to be drawn from these first five experiments varying the pre-session contact between subjects is clear. Minimal contact which merely permits visual or verbal idenfication of one's partner has little effect on the likelihood that subjects will cooperate under risk. They behave very much as they would if they remained completely anonymous. On the other hand, long-standing relationships outside the laboratory do have a marked effect on behavior. Most close friends and married couples were eventually cooperative. Not unexpectedly, in these cases behavior in the laboratory apparently reflects the cooperative relationships outside it.

The relative ineffectiveness of pre-session communication in increasing the amount of cooperation under risk provides further support for our interpretation of the results of the first communication experiments, reported in Chapter 5. There the simultaneous introduction of communication and risk prior to conflict typically led to agreements to cooperate, and these agreements were usually kept. The absence of similar amounts of cooperation in the present pre-session communication experiment suggests that agreements, not merely social contact, are the more important variable in promoting cooperation.

PART III: THE INVOCATION OF GROUP NORMS

For a sociologist the relationship between people is defined by more than the specific content of their past interaction. Roles and group memberships define the ways in which we relate to each other as surely as emotions and shared experiences. A doctor and a patient seeing each other for "business reasons" have more of a relationship than strangers, although they may have never met before. Elements of their interaction are predictable, and their assumptions about each other partly specified. Similarly, two Americans accidentally meeting abroad immediately have more than an empty relationship. They are undoubtedly comrades of a kind, expected to assist each other in trouble, and to understand each other's problems. They are also expected to adhere to similar sets of cultural norms.

In this section we report on two experiments which involve this normative factor. The experiments grew out of our concern with the basic response of our college student subjects to the original larger-risk experiments. We were surprised that the students would be so ready to steal from one another—for that is what they were doing when they "took." Such stealing is obviously a violation of one of the more self-consciously held norms in our society, at least at the verbal level. Parents and other socializing agents presumably work hard at teaching their children not to steal. But the great majority of our subjects stole.

Can we conclude that the norms against stealing were not widely held by our subjects? Were they willing to behave "immorally" as long as there were no probable sanctions? Or was the problem simply that in the absence of communication they did not recognize the applicability of the norm to this situation? Perhaps the "laboratory" and the fact that they had no social relationship with the other person except through a panel of lights and buzzers served to suspend everyday norms and emphasize game playing instead? Thus the situation may not have given off cues which enabled the subjects to translate taking into stealing.

Invoking Outside Norms: The "Steal" Experiment

The solution, we thought, might simply be to point out to the subjects that they were both members of a society that condemned stealing and that the behavior called taking violated this norm. All we had to do was tell them that the experiment was about stealing, that we wanted to know why and when people violated this societally agreed upon norm, and rename the take button the "steal button." We believed it likely that these changes in the instructions would create "demand characteristics" for the experiment which would be conducive to cooperation and restraint from stealing.

METHOD

Six male and six female pairs of subjects were studied using the simplified setting. Procedures were identical to those of the risk experiment, except that portions of the instructions were changed. Included was the following opening statement:

> *One of the most important in our society has always been the question of stealing. People seem to steal from one another quite often. Perhaps you, yourself, have been the victim of a theft. All this stealing goes on despite the fact that everyone agrees that stealing is unethical and immoral. The society spends a lot of money trying to deter people from stealing, with police and other methods, and parents spend a lot of time and emotion trying to teach their children that stealing is bad. Still people steal. That is what this experiment is about— stealing. We are going to give both of you the opportunity to steal from each other and see what you do. What you are going to be able to steal is money that you earn in the experiment. So, before we let you steal, we are going to show you how to earn money.*

Similarly, the description of the take button was changed to:

> *Now that you have both earned some money we can move on to the important part of the experiment—the part where you have a chance to take advantage of the other person. The way you steal money in this experiment is by pressing the remaining button on your little box. We call this the "steal" button. When you press the steal button, please hold for a few seconds. You will then steal one dollar—300 points—from the other person and give 300 points to yourself.*

All further references to the "take button" or "taking" in the instructions were replaced with the terms "steal button" and "stealing."

RESULTS

Unexpectedly, the "steal" instructions had no discernible effect on subject behavior. As Table 7-3 shows, only two

Table 7-3

Summary of Effects: Norm Salience Experiments

	Steal		Exploit	
Pattern	n	%	n	%
Eventual cooperation				
Cooperation without taking	2	17	4	33
Delayed cooperation without taking			1	8
Taking followed by cooperation			1	8
Eventual noncooperation				
Noncooperation without taking	1	8		
Taking and noncooperation	9	75	6	50
Total:	12	100	12	99

of 12 pairs (one male, one female) cooperated, compared with three of 20 in the original replication. For the sample as a whole, risk explained 70% of the variance in the proportion of cooperative responses (means: baseline .99; risk .18). Simply calling attention to the norm clearly did not work.

Using Community Norms: The Rip-Off Experiment

But why hadn't the instructions had an effect? Maybe we had failed to select the stimulus to make the appropriate norms salient. Our introduction of the "steal" instructions had been based on the assumption that any reasonable stimulus which brought the norm into the situation would change the behavior. The assumption had proven incorrect.

We decided to consider more carefully the factors that may be presumed to make norms salient. Surprisingly, little research has focused on the problem since Charters and Newcomb's well-known research with college students (Charters & Newcomb, 1958). Their study emphasized the importance of reference groups for norm salience. Remind the subjects that they are members of the group that holds the specified norm. Perhaps our problem was that we had not specified the correct reference group.

A look at the "steal" instructions reveals that the reference group invoked was American society as a whole. Perhaps this isn't a particularly meaningful reference group for our subjects. What then would be? Since the subjects were all students, we turned to the college student community. To support our invocation of that societal subgroup and their norms, we took advantage of the fact that the group has an unconventional language of its own. The lingo-slang-newspeak of youth is as much a badge of membership as clothes and hair. So "stealing" became "ripping off"

and "exploiting." "Society" became the "student community." The "steal button" became the "exploit button."
The study became one of "under what conditions students
take advantage of each other."

METHOD

Six male and six female pairs were studied under conditions identical to those in the "steal" experiment, except
that the portions of the instructions were rewritten, beginning:

*One of the most important problems in our society has
aways been man's exploitation of other men. This often
occurs when one steals the legitimate earnings that the
other has worked for. Perhaps you, yourself, have been
the victim of a theft. For quite a while now the student
community has prided itself on its closeness and on the
trustworthiness of its members. Recently though, there
has been quite a bit of talk that students on campus have
been increasingly ripping off one another. Stereo sets,
money, records, even clothes have disappeared. More
and more students have become very concerned about
these acts by their community members. There have
been vigilante groups formed by students to catch the
people responsible.*

*This experiment is an attempt to find out under what
conditions students take advantage of one another. We
are going to give both of you students the opportunity to
exploit each other and see whether or not you do. You will
be able to take advantage of each other by stealing the
money that you earn in the experiment. But before we
show you how to exploit each other, we are going to
show you how to earn the money.*

The take button was now introduced with:

> *Now that you have both earned some money we can move on to the important part of the experiment–the part where you have a chance to take advantage of the other person. You do this by pressing the remaining button on your little box. We call this the "exploit" button. When you press the exploit button, please hold for a few seconds. You will then steal $1—300 points—from the other person and give 300 points to yourself.*

Further references to "taking" and the "take button" were now replaced by "exploiting" and the "exploit button."

RESULTS

As Table 7-3 shows, the "rip-off" instructions were partially successful in reducing taking and increasing cooperation among our subjects. Half of all pairs (three female, three male) were eventually cooperative, a proportion significantly greater than in both the original "take" and "steal" conditions.[3] For the sample as a whole, risk explained 21% of the proportion of cooperative responses (means: baseline .99, risk .50).

Although these results support the efficacy of reference groups for making norms salient—for they do seem to have an effect on behavior—they do *not* repudiate all of our fears concerning the norms of the student population. Considering the rates of petty theft common in student living areas, these results might only reflect the realities of everyday behavior.

---

[3] $p < .005$, Fisher Exact Probability test.

The Demand Characteristics of the Instructions

Besides their import for the main hypothesis, the data also have relevance for another current issue. In learning the mechanics of experimenting, one is warned to avoid any "demand characteristics" in the instructions. The argument goes that if subjects know what the experimenter wants, they will try to please him by behaving appropriately. Even subtle hints and facial gestures may give the experimenter's wishes away (the well-known "experimenter bias" effect). Therefore, keep the setting impersonal. If possible, keep the experimenters unaware of the hypotheses and the treatment for a particular subject. In one sense our results may be seen as supporting such warnings. The differences between the "steal" and "rip-off" treatments are subtle and were contained fully in the instructions (rather than in conditions). And the subjects behaved differently. Demand characteristics *can* affect behavior. On the other hand, compare the effects of the "take" and "steal" treatments. We purposely designed the "steal" treatment to convey important demand characteristics—and it failed to affect the subjects. Thus the findings illustrate the importance of demand characteristics *and* the strength of situational contingencies. It can be as misleading to overestimate as to underestimate demand effects.

PART IV: INEQUITY AND INTERPERSONAL RISK

Finally we come full circle. The first independent variable we considered for its impact on cooperation was inequity. We found that it tended to reduce cooperation even in the face of economic incentives to cooperate. In explaining our initial focus on inequity, we noted that it was a product of a relationship between two partners who might cooperate. Inequity, as we have used it, requires a comparison.

We have not forgotten this relationship. So in a chapter on relationships, we decided to investigate what effect inequitable relations between partners might have on the likelihood of cooperation under large risk. We have some suggestive evidence from Chapter 3. There, the opportunity to transfer in the moderate inequity condition was the condition we later studied as "small risk" in Chapter 4. With inequity and the opportunity to take, most pairs eventually cooperated and transferred to equity. But would the same result occur if both the inequity and risk were large? Separately, both large risk and large inequity produced more disruption than small risk and moderate inequity. Thus if the extreme conditions together produce appreciable amounts of cooperation, we would have additional evidence of a very substantial interaction effect between the two variables.

METHOD

Five male and five female pairs were studied for four sessions in the sequence of conditions shown in Table 7-4. As in the case of both the original inequity and large-risk experiments, the standard setting and procedures were used.

RESULTS AND DISCUSSION

Results strongly support the interaction effect between inequity and risk. Seven of the 10 pairs (four male, three female) eventually cooperated when the opportunity to take accompanied inequity, a proportion significantly greater than under large risk alone.[4] For the sample as a whole, inequity and risk explained only 10% of the variance in

---

[4] $p < .005$, Fisher Exact Probability test.

Table 7-4

Conditions Defining Inequity–Risk Experiment

Session		Segment	Counts[a]			Minutes in segment
			Cooperation		Individual	
			A	B		
1	1–4	Training				
2	5	Baseline: Cooperation or individual responding	4	4	3	30
	6	Inequity and risk: inequitable cooperation with taking or individual responding	20	4	3	90
3	7	Baseline	4	4	3	30
	8	Inequity–risk	20	4	3	90
4	9	Baseline	4	4	3	30
	10	Inequity–risk	20	4	3	90

[a] Each count was worth .1¢.

the proportion of cooperative responses (means: baseline 1.00; inequity–risk .70).

As Table 7-5 shows, six pairs eventually cooperated with transfers, although in three of these pairs, bilateral taking preceded transfer. By the final session, taking was used only by the underpaid subject in five of the pairs to greatly reduce or eliminate the inequity. In the sixth pair subjects met after the second session and agreed to split the earnings evenly—a solution having the same effect as the underpaid subject's taking.

Only one pair cooperated without transfer. Cooperation began in Session 3, following taking by both subjects. Although the overpaid subject would not let his partner reduce the inequity by taking, the underpaid subject continued to cooperate.

Table 7-5

Summary of Effects: Inequity–Risk Experiment

Pattern	n	%
Eventual cooperation		
Taking followed by cooperation with transfer	3	30
Cooperation with transfer	3[a]	30
Taking followed by cooperation	1	10
Eventual noncooperation		
Taking and noncooperation	2	20
Cooperation disrupted by taking	1	10
Total:	10	100

[a]Includes pair who agreed to split earnings after the experiment.

Of the three eventually noncooperative pairs, two pairs made no cooperative responses with taking available. Taking occurred in each risk segment in one pair and in all but the final segment in the other. One pair was cooperative initially without taking, but ceased cooperating in Session 3 following taking by both subjects.

Inequity in cooperative rewards thus seems to redefine the risk situation for many of the subjects. Under reward equity most subjects use the take opportunity to exploit, while under inequity the opportunity to take is apparently a stimulus that evokes responses to restore equity.

The higher incidence of cooperation in the present experiment, however, may also have been due in part to another factor besides inequity. The total cooperative reward for each pair exceeded that available in any previous risk experiment. Cooperating pairs received a total of 24 counts compared with six counts in the large-risk experiment and 18 counts in the large-risk, large-pay experiment.

With the 24 counts divided equally, subjects received three more counts than in the large-risk, large-pay variation. Still, the proportion of pairs cooperating with the large-risk and large-pay was less than half that in the present experiment.

CHAPTER 8

ACHIEVING COOPERATION
UNDER RISK: PACIFISM

After more than 25 experiments investigating the behavior of subjects under risk, one conclusion is clear: In
the absence of some means of mediating or avoiding risk,
our population of college students was rarely able to avoid
conflict and the ultimate destruction of a cooperative
relationship. Even subjects who did not initiate taking
were for the most part all too willing to retaliate following
a take by their partner.

This propensity, however, does not preclude all

response strategies from successfully promoting cooperation. It simply indicates that such strategies were rarely
used in our sample of subjects. In this chapter we will consider one possible exception to the rule of strategic failure
in the promotion of cooperation. Where in the previous
two chapters we have been concerned with the manipulation
of relationships and contingencies by the experimenter
in order to achieve cooperation, we will now consider
what a participant might do if he steadfastly seeks to make
his group cooperative.

The strategy we have selected for attention derives in
part from one regularity in behavior which emerged from
the previous experiments. In those few pairs which did
maintain cooperation under high risk conditions, it was
most often the case that neither subject took. In other words,
cooperation typically depended upon the total absence of
taking. This finding, it could be argued, provides evidence
that a strategy of "pacifism" could facilitate cooperation,
where pacifism implies both cooperation and an uncondi-
tional refusal to take.

Unfortunately, our previous results do not provide
clear evidence that the subjects in cooperative pairs were
in fact "pacifists." Since no taking occurred, these subjects
may simply have been unwilling to initiate taking. They
may have readily retaliated if taken from. Thus, the most
we can say from our cooperative pairs is that a refusal
to initiate taking promotes cooperation. Despite their
inconclusiveness, however, these findings are consistent
with the notion that pacifism might be an effective strategy
for promoting cooperation. As such, they differ from the
general thrust of previous experimental research, which
has not supported the efficacy of "pacifist" strategies for
cooperation in potentially conflictive situations.

Evidence on the effects of pacifism derives from the
number of studies in which a confederate uses an uncon-

ditionally cooperative strategy while playing a variation of a Prisoner's Dilemma (for a review see Oskamp, 1971) or bargaining game (Shure, Meeker, and Hansford, 1965). Ofshe, in summarizing this research, reaches the following pessimistic conclusion:

> ... it has been found that in a situation of conflict of interest between two individuals, the progessive disclosure of one individual's moral position as a pacifist ... (has) the effect of producing either no substantial change in his opponent's aggressive behavior or result(s) in increased aggression [Ofshe, 1971, p. 264].

Vinacke (1969), reviewing the data on the effects of using *any* programmed strategy, such as pacifism, in game situations states that "in general, such procedures are unsuccessful in influencing subjects." Although significant results are sometimes obtained, the differences reported are rarely substantial, and almost certainly not impressive enough to convince anyone that a pacifist strategy should be recommended as a means of avoiding conflict and increasing cooperation.

The five experiments reported in this chapter explore the effects of pacifism in the large-risk setting. Four experiments examine a series of variations on a pacifist strategy using the simplified setting and Norwegian subjects. The fifth experiment is a cross-cultural replication using American subjects.

Unconditional Cooperation: The Total Pacifism Experiment

The first experiment was designed to investigate the effect of a totally pacifist strategy enacted by one subject on the likelihood of cooperation. Since the risk situation typically leads to conflict and noncooperation, and research in other settings does not support the effectiveness of pacifist strategies in mitigating conflict, we expected that at best a moderate change in behavior would occur.

METHOD

Subjects were seven female and eight male University of Oslo student volunteers. With the exception of the programmed play of a confederate, all aspects of the experiment were identical to those of the cross-cultural replication experiment with Norwegian subjects reported in Chapter 5.

Confederates used in the experiment were of the same sex as the subjects and were students at the University of Oslo as well. The confederates were treated by the experimenter as if they were naive subjects. During the training segments confederates played "perfectly" in order to maximize rewards. Under the baseline and risk conditions, the confederates were totally cooperative, at all times leaving the task selection switch set to work together. During the risk condition the confederates never pressed the take button.

RESULTS

Thirteen of the 15 pairs met the criteria during the training and baseline sequence. Two pairs (one female and one male) failed to cooperate during the baseline and were not studied further.

Cooperation. A pacifist strategy was highly effective in eventually producing cooperation under risk. Faced with a totally pacifist partner, 12 of 13 subjects (six male, six female) themselves continued to cooperate or to eventually reestablish cooperation, a proportion significantly greater than in the Norway replication with no confederate.[1] **All** 12 subjects were cooperating continuously by the ninety-first trial; the median subject became cooperative by the eighth trial. For the sample as a whole, risk explained only 4% of the variance in the proportion of cooperative responses (means: baseline 1.00, risk .92).

Taking and Cooperation.   The various patterns of taking and cooperation are shown in Table 8-1. Seven of the subjects were totally nonexploitative, never taking from the confederate. Two of these were totally cooperative, while five were cooperative after a delay.

Five subjects took from the confederate early, but eventually ceased taking and became totally cooperative. Two of these subjects took once, two took twice, and one took four times. The latest any take occurred was on trial 40.

Finally, one subject continuously exploited the confederate. He took 13 times in all, with the last take coming on trial 184. The earnings at the end of the risk segment showed the confederate with only 32 points, while the subject had taken over 700 points away.

DISCUSSION

In this situation pacifism clearly worked as a strategy for producing cooperation. First, the pacifist stance brought about cooperation in subjects whose main reason for not cooperating was apparently the risk of being exploited. When these subjects eventually switched to cooperation and were not exploited, cooperation emerged. Of the five subjects who began the risk session on the individual task and who did not themselves take from the confederates, only one continued to stay on the individual task through-

[1] $p < .05$, Fisher Exact Probability Test.

Table 8-1

Summary of Effects: Pacifism Experiments

	Total pacifism (Norwegian)		Pacifism following 10-trial delay (Norwegian)		Pacifism following 30-trial delay (Norwegian)		Pacifism following conflict (Norwegian)		Total pacifism (American)	
Pattern[a]	n	%	n	%	n	%	n	%	n	%
Eventual cooperation										
Cooperation without taking	2	15			3	23			5	25
Delayed cooperation without taking	5	38	5	50	1	8			3	15
Taking followed by cooperation	5	38	3	30	3	23	7	54	2	10
Cooperation and taking									1	5
Eventual noncooperation										
Taking and noncooperation	1	8	2	20	5	38	6	46	8	40
Noncooperation without taking					1	8			1	5
Total:	13	99	10	100	13	100	13	100	20	100

[a]In delay experiments, pattern refers to naive subjects' behavior after the delay.

out the risk segment. The others eventually tried cooperation. Second, the classic pattern of "turning the other cheek"
to aggression eventually worked on several subjects who
began by taking from the confederate. Despite the continuing possibilities for exploitation, these subjects ceased
taking and reciprocated the cooperation.

Defining the Situation: Two Delayed-Pacifism Experiments

The results suggesting that pacifism can reverse the
behavior of an exploiter are particularly relevant to the
central assumptions of pacifism. For our own work, however, the fact that more than half of all subjects never exploited the confederate in this situation raises a somewhat
different question. In our previous experiments almost
all "real" pairs experienced some taking. It would be statistically unusual to obtain this result if, in fact, half of
all individual subjects would not take first. This could
only occur if the nonexploitative subjects were almost always
paired with exploitative ones—an unlikely occurrence.

One possible reason for this disparity may be the
communication effect of *delays* in cooperation caused by
working on the individual task. In other words, in a "real"
pair both subjects may begin with the least risky strategy—
working individually. This behavior may communicate a
potential exploitativeness to their partners, eventually
resulting in conflict. It would seem likely that any implication of exploitativeness would be greater the longer the
delay. Thus the two experiments reported below consider
the effects on cooperation of short and long delays in insti-
tuting a pacifist strategy.

Subjects and Procedures.   All procedures were identical
to those of the previous experiment with the following

exceptions: In the short-delay experiment, the confederate set his task selection switch to the individual task at the beginning of the risk segment, and switched to the totally cooperative strategy on trial 11. In the long-delay experiment, the confederate waited until trial 31 before switching to cooperation.

Subjects were five male and five female University of Oslo students in the short-delay experiment, and seven female and six male students in the long-delay experiment.

RESULTS AND DISCUSSION

Short Delay. As Table 8-1 shows, a 10-trial delay by the confederate before switching to the cooperative task produced results similar to those from the previous pacifism experiment where no delay was used. At the conclusion of the risk condition, eight of the 10 subjects (four male, four female) were cooperating. For the sample as a whole, risk explained 11% of the variance in the proportion of cooperative responses (means: baseline 1.00, risk .80).

Long Delay. In contrast to the 10-trial delay, a 30-trial delay by the confederate before switching to cooperation reduced but did not eliminate the effects of pacifism. As Table 8-1 shows, seven of the 13 pairs (four male, three female) eventually cooperated, a proportion significantly lower than with total pacifism[2] but still greater than in the Norway replication with no confederate.[3] For the sample as a whole, risk explained 31% of the variance in the proportion of cooperative responses (means: baseline 1.00, risk .54).

The results of the long-delay experiment support the notion that the effectiveness of total pacifism may have

[2] $p < .05$, Fisher Exact Probability Test.

[3] $p < .05$, x^2 Test.

been in part dependent upon the communication inherent in a totally cooperative strategy. A 30-trial delay apparently served as a stimulus indicating to the subject that his partner (the confederate) at least *might* take. In contrast, total cooperation made a nonaggressive propensity evident. Apparently the short 10-trial delay was more like total cooperation in this respect.

Reducing Hostilities: The Pacifism Conflict Experiment

The previous experiments indicated that a substantial delay in beginning a totally pacifist strategy may undermine the communication inherent in such a position. In some situations, however, the situation preceding pacifism may be even less conducive to cooperation. Before deciding on a pacifist strategy, the actor may already have committed some aggressive act, and a conflictive relationship may have been established. In this experiment, we investigated the extent to which such a "contaminated" situation works against the efficacy of pacifism.

METHOD

Subjects were six female and seven male University of Oslo students. Procedures were identical to those of the total pacifism experiment, except that the confederate *took* from the subject on trial 1, or on the first trial on which the subject switched to work together. For all trials the confederate remained switched to work together. Following his single take on the first possible trial, he never took again.

RESULTS AND DISCUSSION

Under risk conditions, the confederate was able to take from the subject by trial 8 in all but two pairs. In these two pairs taking occurred on the 23rd and 28th trials.

Taking substantially reduced the effectiveness of pacifism. As Table 8-1 shows, seven of the 13 subjects (four male, three female) eventually cooperated, a proportion significantly lower than with total pacifism[4] but still greater than in the Norway replication with no confederate.[5] For the sample as a whole, risk explained 32% of the variance in the proportion of cooperative responses (means: baseline 1.00; risk .55).

Cooperation began by trial 47 for all but one of the seven eventually cooperative subjects. Three of these pairs took once—enough to make the rewards equal, and never took again. The other four had from two to six takes. All six noncooperative subjects were exploitative. The total number of takes ranged from three to 10.

Thus two confederate responses prior to pacifism, taking and the long delay before cooperation, were similar in the degree to which they reduced the effectiveness of pacifism. It is particularly interesting that simply a reluctance to cooperate was as consequential as exploitation in affecting future cooperation.

A Cross-Cultural Replication: The American Pacifism Experiment

Earlier we demonstrated that the basic effect of risk on cooperation was replicable cross-culturally. Risk destroyed cooperation in all 12 "real" (no confederate) Norwegian pairs, and in 17 of 20 "real" American pairs. The question we now ask is whether the effects of pacifism are similar as well. The experiment reported below was a cross-cultural

[4] $p < .05$, Fisher Exact Probability Test.

[5] $p < .01$, Fisher Exact Probability Test.

replication of the total pacifism experiment, using American rather than Norwegian subjects.

METHOD

Procedures were identical to those described for the total pacifism experiment, with two exceptions: instructions were in English, and each point was worth one-third of a cent. Subjects were 10 male and 10 female students.

RESULTS

As Table 8-1 shows, the results do not fully replicate those of the Norwegian pacifism experiment. Instead of cooperation emerging in nearly every pair, only 11 of the 20 subjects (eight female, three male) eventually became cooperative. For the sample as a whole, risk explained 27% of the variance in the proportion of cooperative responses (means: baseline .98; risk .58). While the proportion of cooperative subjects is significantly lower than the 12 of 13 in the Norwegian sample,[6] it is still significantly higher than the two of 20 American (real) pairs who cooperated in the original replication.[7]

Interestingly, the major difference between American and Norwegian subjects seems to lie not in the proportion of subjects who took, but in the proportion who ceased taking and began to cooperate. Taking occurred in six of 13 (46%) Norwegian and 11 of 20 (55%) American pairs. However, taking ceased in five of the Norwegian pairs but in only two of the American pairs. The lack of cooperation following taking by Americans is consonant with previous findings on "real" pairs of Americans in both the standard

[6] $p < .05$, Fisher Exact Probability Test.

[7] $p < .05$, x^2 Test.

and simplified settings, where cooperation tended to emerge only when there was *no* taking.

DISCUSSION

Thus the extreme effect of pacifism on cooperation found with Norwegian subjects does not appear to generalize to Americans. Why? It may be that American culture is generally more supportive of exploitative behavior. Or, Americans may be more likely to interpret ambiguous situations in terms of conflict. Another possibility is that the reward difference between cooperation and individual work, although sufficient to maintain cooperation when no other factors interfered, did not mean as much to the presumably wealthier American subjects. Thus cooperation itself may have been a less sought-after pattern of behavior. Finally, American experimental subjects may be more sensitive to the possibility that they are being duped. As Kelman (1967) and others have pointed out, a very large number of experiments which include deception have been performed on American subjects. This has probably affected the subject pool, making it wary. In this experiment, one can only be made the fool by trusting and being exploited.

Deciding among these explanations would, of course, require further and extensive research. The differences between Norwegians and Americans, however, should not mask the most important common fact—pacifism did have an effect on behavior in both samples. For Americans in particular, this contrasts with previous research, where exploitation has seemed to be the most likely response to pacifism.

Conclusions: Comparison with Previous Research

Pacifism, it seems, can work. However, in terms of the variables examined here, how well it works appears to de-

pend on at least three factors: the communication of pacifist intent, the previous level of conflict in the relationship,
and the societal background of the participants. Each of
these factors distinguish our results from those of previous
research.

The most obvious effect is that of societal differences.
Almost all previous research was done with American
subjects, where, according to our results, the effects of
pacifism seem to be less pronounced. However, since even
with American subjects pacifism did have a substantial
effect, differences must also obtain in the other factors.

There are important differences between the current
setting and procedures and those used in previous research.
We have previously noted the inherent ambiguity of intent
in the Prisoner's Dilemma. There the noncooperative
choice is both safer—one minimizes one's loss—and more
aggressive—one's partner receives his maximum loss if he
chooses to cooperate. In the present risk setting, by contrast, self-protection and taking are topologically distinct.
Thus if subjects initially choose to act conservatively by
withdrawing from cooperation, they do not necessarily
exploit a partner who cooperates. In the bargaining task
used by Shure, Meeker, and Hansford (1965), an alter-
nating strategy was required for cooperation—a solution
that may have been less obvious to subjects than the well-
practiced cooperative response in the risk setting.

Apart from the ambiguity or complexity of the various
cooperative contingencies, there is an additional variable
which also may be important—the size of loss that is in-
curred if the other player exploits. In his theoretical
paper on the sources of cooperation and conflict, Deutsch
(1962) also focuses on this variable in distinguishing between risk-taking (gambling) and trusting behavior. In
both cases the individual is choosing a path with an ambiguous outcome—he may either profit or lose. However,

"one gambles when one has much to gain or *little to lose* [italics
added] and one trusts when one has *much to lose* [italics

added] or little to gain. Hence, one does not need much confidence in a positive outcome to gamble, but one needs considerable confidence in a positive outcome to trust [Deutsch, 1962; p. 304]."

In these terms, the current situation is one in which there is much to lose—the choice to cooperate is one predominantly of "trust." In the Prisoner's Dilemma, by contrast, there is comparatively little to lose from a single cooperative response. Thus the choice is one of "risk-taking." Which consequences a cooperative choice entails may determine the reaction to the choice. Where cooperation entails large possible losses, the question of trust becomes paramount, and communication of trustworthiness on the part of the other player is of prime importance. Where cooperation entails little loss, a gambling atmosphere may prevail. Some taking is likely to occur, setting up conflictive relations. Pacifism is treated as a bad gambling tactic and a misunderstanding of the situation by the other player, rather than as communicating trustworthiness.

Finally, we should note one further implication if the size of potential loss is important for the effectiveness of pacifism. The larger this loss, the less one might be entitled to say that pacifism worked, even when most subjects finally cooperated. When the loss is large enough, such as the loss of one's life, even a 99% effectiveness in producing cooperation might not lead us to conclude that we wish to employ a pacifist strategy. Ninety-nine to one odds may just not be good enough.

CHAPTER 9

CONCLUSIONS AND SPECULATIONS

We will begin by summarizing the more than 30 experiments which comprise the bulk of the preceding chapters,
thereby at once juxtaposing the results of materials previously discussed separately and providing a convenient
review of the main findings and concerns of the research.
Table 9-1 contains data from each experiment selected as
most relevant for these purposes: the number of pairs
meeting baseline criteria for retention in the sample, the
proportion of these pairs cooperating at the conclusion of
the experimental treatment, the proportion of cooperative

175

Table 9-1

Summary of Effects

Condition	Number cooperating when rewards favor cooperation (Baseline N)	% of Baseline N cooperating at conclusion of condition[a] (number in parentheses)	Mean proportion of cooperative responses during baseline	Mean proportion of cooperative responses in period prior to termination of condition[b]	% of variance in proportion of cooperative responses explained by condition (eta²)
INEQUITY					
Large inequity	10	60 (6)	.98	.62	23
Moderate inequity	20	90 (18)	.98	.84	10
Small inequity	20	100 (20)	.94	.97	07
Moderate inequity with transfer by giving	10	80 (8)	.99	.84	10
Moderate inequity with transfer by taking	10	90 (9)	.94	.91	01
Replication with children	12	83 (10)	.88	.67	12
INTERPERSONAL RISK: EFFECTS OF SIZE AND GENERALITY					
Small risk	32	53 (17)	.96	.56	25
Large risk	28	7 (2)	.95	.09	81
Large-risk, extended	7	14 (1)	.98	.12	80
Large-risk, large-pay	9	33 (3)	.93	.33	43
Large-risk destroy	8	88 (7)	.98	.86	06
Intermittent risk	5	0 (0)	.99	.18	87
Asymmetric risk	15	27 (4)	.98	.34	50
Simplified risk setting	20	15 (3)	.98	.15	68
Norway replication	12	0 (0)	.98	.00	98
Mixed-sex replication	20	30 (6)	.99	.33	51

[a]A pair was categorized as cooperative if the percentage of cooperative responses during the final 30 minutes (or 40 trials) of the condition was 80% of that during the baseline.

[b]Mean proportion of cooperative responses during the final 30 minutes (or 40 trials) of the condition.

[c]Excludes pairs who were cooperative with risk only.

Table 9-1 (Cont'd)

Summary of Effects

Condition	Number cooperating when rewards favor cooperation (Baseline N)	% of Baseline N cooperating at conclusion of condition[a] (number in parentheses)	Mean proportion of cooperative responses during baseline	Mean proportion of cooperative responses in period prior to termination of condition[b]	% of variance in proportion of cooperative responses explained by condition (eta^2)
ACHIEVING COOPERATION UNDER RISK					
Protection and communication					
No protection	6	67 (4)	.99	.66	19
Signaled avoidance	5[c]	100 (5)	.99	.99	02
Free-operant avoidance	5[c]	100 (5)	1.00	1.00	0
Communication	12	75 (9)	.99	.77	13
Communication delay	9[c]	56 (5)	.97	.44	36
Relations between People					
Presession visibility	10	10 (1)	.98	.10	82
Presession communication	20	20 (4)	.97	.20	65
Visibility	20	20 (4)	.99	.20	66
Married couples	4	10 (4)	1.00	1.00	0
Friends	20	65 (13)	.98	.68	18
"Steal" instructions	12	17 (2)	.99	.18	70
"Rip-off" instructions	12	50 (6)	.99	.50	21
Inequity–risk	10	70 (7)	1.00	.70	10
Pacifism					
Total pacifism (Norwegian)	13	92 (12)	1.00	.92	04
Pacifism following 10-trial delay (Norwegian)	10	80 (8)	1.00	.80	11
Pacifism following 30-trial delay (Norwegian)	13	54 (7)	1.00	.54	31
Pacifism following conflict (Norwegian)	13	54 (7)	1.00	.55	32
Total pacifism (American)	20	55 (11)	.98	.58	27

responses by the sample under baseline and treatment conditions, and the amount of variance in cooperation explained by the treatment (eta^2).

At the most general level, we have argued that these data support acceptance of two basic factors which influence the appearance and maintenance of cooperation in dyads: inequity and interpersonal risk.

Inequity

The impact of inequity is less strong and conclusive. The basic effects of inequity on cooperation may be summarized as follows:

1. Some persons withdrew from an inequitably rewarded cooperative task to a less profitable individual one.

2. The number of pairs withdrawing from cooperation and the extent of each pair's withdrawal increased with inequity size.

3. When the inequity was moderate or large, withdrawal from cooperation was initiated by the underpaid subject.

4. Removal of the inequity for noncooperative pairs generally led to the resumption of cooperation.

5. Providing a means of reward transfer (either giving or taking) generally led to cooperation in pairs who were noncooperative when transfer was not available, and led to some disruption in previously cooperative pairs if no transfers were made.

6. When the opportunity to take a large amount ($1) was introduced with a large inequity, taking emerged as a means of transfer rather than disruption.

These findings are in keeping with a considerable amount of previous theory regarding the importance of inequity in human interaction, and substantiate other research which indicates that inequity affects various types of behavior. In the literature on cooperation, however, inequity has tended to be paired with nonprofitability, even loss, on the part of the underpaid partner (Pritchard, 1969). On the other hand, some widely cited nonlaboratory examples of inequity have not been characterized by this relationship, e.g., alienation among well-paid soldiers in World War II (Merton, 1957). Situations in which the inequitably rewarded task is also the more profitable one for the participants provides the severest test for inequity's effects.

It should be noted that while our results clearly suggest the disruptive effects of inequity for at least some subjects, they provide little general evidence as to the disruptive force of inequity in social relations. In any setting, reward differences that accrue over time are a function both of the size of each reward and the number of rewarded responses. In our experiments, variations were made only in the former, and the proportional differences between rewards far exceeded those customarily cited in nonlaboratory settings. On the other hand, the number of responses (or the length of time under inequitable conditions) hardly approached that outside of the laboratory. Furthermore, any patterns of behavior produced by inequity in our setting reflect responses to inequity learned elsewhere—presumably in the socialization histories of the subjects. The degree to which persons of various backgrounds respond differently to similar situations of inequity has not been investigated.

The recognition of the potential effects of inequity has already spawned a substantial speculative literature of "real-life" examples: the well-paid veteran who won't block for the overpriced rookie, the faculty colleague who feels himself unappreciated and underpaid and thus withdraws from collective efforts, the marriage which fails when the wife feels she is being exploited by the husband, etc. Thus, in part, the inequity findings have confirmed for a specific form of behavior what many would expect to be true. Therefore, instead of expanding the list of analogous situations, we will focus on several specific points which were, perhaps, less predictable.

One noteworthy aspect of the findings is that withdrawal from the inequitable situation occurred despite the fact that the source of the inequity was impersonal—certainly not the work of the overpaid partner, and seemingly random in the selection of who was favored and who disfavored. The harm done to the overpaid by the underpaid partner when he ceased cooperating to avoid inequity—and harm there certainly was in a loss of potential earnings—was therefore directed at an "innocent party."

Also of note is the finding that inequity seemed to justify the expropriation of the overpaid subject's money by his underpaid partner. When inequity was combined with interpersonal risk, underpaid subjects used the taking mechanism to make up much of the inequity. Most overpaid partners permitted taking to the point of equity, and both partners continued to cooperate. Thus taking became a means for rectifying inequities rather than a mode of conflict. It may well be that analogous, often more subtle, compensatory behaviors are common in other enterprises where one member feels he has a better "deal" than his partner(s). For example, husbands, sensing that societal sexism gives them greater rewards, may allow exploitation by their wives in unequal consumption patterns—as a form of compensation. Businesses characterized as paternalistic frequently pay lower employees less but may be more tolerant of activities that could be grounds for dismissal.

Interpersonal Risk

The more conclusive results of this research concern the effects of interpersonal risk. In a series of mutually supportive studies, we have demonstrated the strength of the impact that risk has on cooperation, and various aspects of the generality of the effect. The basic effects using isolated subjects can be summarized as follows:

1. The addition of interpersonal risk to cooperation typically produced taking, then withdrawal to the less profitable individual task. Disruption was substantial when the risk was small, almost total when the risk was large.

2. Removal of risk generally led to the resumption of cooperation.

3. The effect of large risk was similar for Norwegian and American subjects.

4. The effect of large risk on cooperation did not change substantially with time.

5. Large risk remained disruptive for the majority of pairs even when (a) the difference in rewards for cooperating and working individually was increased threefold; (b) risk was present as little as 7% of the time when subjects were cooperating; and (c) only one subject in each pair was able to take.

6. Large risk did not appreciably disrupt cooperation when taking did not reward the taker.

At the level of the group response, the control exercised by the manipulation of risk was almost complete when subjects were isolated. However, on the individual level there were a variety of behavior patterns which culminated in withdrawal. One principle, though, can be used to explain most of the eventual disruption: Subjects faced with a choice of responses initially made the one that was followed by the largest immediate reward. The most profitable single response—taking—occurred in most pairs soon after it was possible. Eventually, at least one of the subjects withdrew to the no-risk individual task, either to protect newly won gains or to avoid further loss. Evidence that the behavior of isolated subjects was in fact a product of the reward structure and not a procedural artifact was shown by the greatly reduced disruption when the rewards for taking were eliminated (destroy experiment).

Dominance of reward maximization was one of the ways in which behavior in the risk situation differed importantly from that in the inequity setting. While reward-maximizing was also evident for a number of pairs under inequity, for some their behavior was also clearly a function of other previously learned social responses. It was not that responses other than early taking were unavailable or even unanticipated under risk. Given the subjects' participation in relations entailing trust outside the laboratory or their understanding of gaming strategies of reward maximization, other obvious behavior patterns such as cooperation without taking or delayed take attempts were expected to be common. They were, in fact, rare.

Mitigating the risk effect. If the strain away from cooperation toward individualism or privatism is severe, spontaneous, long-standing cooperation still exists. It survives with sufficient frequency that we know the effects of risk to be mitigated substantially in many concrete situations. This research has identified some of the characteristics of situations that might serve this purpose. Channels of communication, usable warnings systems, and certain types of past relations are examples of objective factors that seem to increase the possibility of sustained cooperation. On the individual level, it was found that a pacifist strategy could induce a substantial number of persons to cooperate in the face of risk. Other factors were examined which did not prove as useful. Visibility, the invocation of moral norms without the successful invocation of group commitments, and making risk intermittent did not foster high rates of cooperation.

As we have noted, some of these variables have also been investigated in previous studies, whose results often did not accurately predict the findings in the present research. However, these studies employed settings and procedures different in many important respects from those we have used. Unique to the present setting was the separation of cooperative, noncooperative (individual), and taking responses, thus permitting the frequencies of each to be observed. Our procedures were designed to minimize behavioral variability attributable to differences between subjects in reinforcer effectiveness and task clarity, and to determine long as well as short-term condition effects. Thus, checks were made as to the efficacy of the reinforcer, training was extensive, and conditions remained in effect until some behavioral stability was evident. From research in various contexts, in particular the Prisoner's Dilemma, it is clear that seemingly minor variations in the setting or procedures can greatly influence the effects of a variable. Hence, it cannot be assumed that variables such as communication, pacifist strategies, or power differentials have a similar effect in settings with "dilemmas," "conflicts," or "risks," simply because the settings share the possibility of being resolved by cooperation. Any relation must be specified far more precisely in terms of response contingencies and salient stimuli.

Structuring the Environment for Cooperative Behavior: Some Implications

To most social psychologists, the preceding experiments fall well within the bounds of basic research—experiments in which isomorphism with settings outside the laboratory is sacrificed for control over socially relevant variables. Some critics might argue that such a choice precludes any serious attempt at establishing the generality of the findings outside of the laboratory. It has been argued that the uniqueness of the laboratory environment and its experimental procedures make the resulting behavior equally unique. However, the lack of what Aronson and Carlsmith (1968) term "mundane realism" is not the primary concern in assessing the potential generality of a relationship. What is crucial is the strength of the relationship and the presence elsewhere of key variables upon which it is contingent. We have seen evidence of the almost total control over cooperation exercised by the possible loss of tangible resources. Such control argues for the presence of what Aronson and Carlsmith (1968) term "experimental realism," which refers to the seriousness with which subjects respond to the experimental contingencies. Strong, replicable relationships between variables in a controlled setting establish the presence of a relationship under at least one set of definable conditions, and thus generality becomes a possibility. Failure to obtain a strong relationship under the same circumstances makes generality questionable, regardless of setting, since either the relationship is inherently weak or the characteristics of the situations in which it holds have yet to be discovered. It is on the basis of their strength and specificity that the present findings differ from those of much previous research, and thus have the potential for generality.

The possibility of generality is, of course, scarcely a substitute for its demonstration. Yet barring a marked increase in the control social scientists can exercise over various societal institutions, immediate systematic replication of the findings in natural settings seems unlikely. Rather than diminishing the importance of laboratory findings, this situation may leave the laboratory as the only place where the relationships between variables can be clearly described. Important real-world analogs to a number of the conditions we have investigated are ubiquitous. Hence, treated in a conservative fashion, the relationships we have described can serve to suggest less obvious sources of problems in ongoing social settings.

As we have noted previously, it is easy to take a pessimistic view of the implications of this research. But such a view may be misleading. Although we began this book by suggesting the value of cooperation, we also noted that we would approach the problem by studying why people do *not* cooperate. And so we have. We have not taken the motivation to cooperate as problematic. Instead, we have simply made cooperation a more effective means to economic rewards, and found, as expected, that this is a reasonable way to evoke cooperation. We assume that much of the real world looks like this. Were there no costs internal to the process, cooperation would be a superior means of solving many of our problems and achieving many of our aspirations. It would work.

What we were seeking were precisely those costs or problems for the process of cooperation—and we found them. Unfortunately, solutions are not the necessary result of identifying the problems. Nevertheless, such knowledge should provide some suggestions as to where one might begin. Our summary of findings at the beginning of this chapter thus stands as well for some factors that might be profitably attended by people considering cooperation, or seeking to structure situations so that others will cooperate. First and foremost, they suggest attention to the elements contained in the cooperative situations that involve pooled resources and thus potential interpersonal risk. What protection is offered from joint access? Can warnings or other protective mechanisms be constructed which would drastically limit the probability of successful exploitation? Strategies employed have ranged from physical threats to electronic surveillance.

Therapists of various persuasions have traditionally decried lack of communication as the source of many conflicts. What are the barriers to communication within a given potentially cooperative setting? Paradoxically, the very discussion of potential mutual exploitation may be culturally prohibited to people arranging a cooperative venture. Raising the question may be a symbol of distrust. So for those who do not trust completely, there is no solution. For example, it has been widely noted that sexual problems are one important source of mutual dissatisfaction in marriage. Patterns of perceived exploitation and uncooperativeness are often mentioned. Perhaps even more common is a taboo on discussing sexual problems between partners, and of reaching "cold-blooded" agreements about a romantic topic. To solve these problems, an institutionalized means of increasing communication may in fact provide a key. So may factors in the culture which directly counter the taboo.

The absolute size of the risk involved is also often subject to manipulation and, in general, should be reduced if cooperation is to be most easily achieved. By size, we mean the injury which can be inflicted from a single act of exploitation. The less costly one exploitative response, the more it is likely that partners will try again to cooperate. A small loss can be more easily ignored or regained, and may instigate the development of protective devices rather than a severance of relations. In short, a shaping process may be required for trust as well as for other forms of learned behavior.

Another relevant factor is the degree of anonymity in the situation. Elsewhere, anonymity has been posited as a key element leading to "deindividuation"—an hypothesized process in which various social conditions produce perceptual changes leading to a lowered threshold of normally restrained behavior (Festinger, Pepitone, & Newcomb, 1952; Singer, Brush, & Lubin, 1965; Cannavale, Scarr & Pepitone, 1970; Zimbardo, 1970). The high incidence of antisocial behaviors of anonymous subjects in the initial large-risk experiment is congruent with the deindividuation paradigm. Unexpected, however, were the conditions of identifiability sufficient to reduce antisocial behavior in the risk setting. Minimal identifiability in the form of mere visibility or brief introduction had little effect. Only some form of social contact, either through communication or past relations, produced effects that differed markedly from the anonymous condition.

Ironically, the thrust of modern society seems to be in the other direction—towards the creation of more and more relationships which are sustained and initiated in relatively impersonal ways. Technology has provided an array of electronic equipment by which relationships can be conducted, frequently with a computer specifying the content of communication. These have opened the range of our relationships, as befits a society in which specialization creates interdependence. But the question remains, are social relations based on such interactions conducive to cooperation? Our results do *not* suggest such an outcome for strangers whose interaction is mediated and even initiated through signals.

But if cooperation is necessary and flourishes best within personal relationships, how do the numerous successful relationships develop in an impersonally structured society? One answer seems to be the development of numerous rituals and arenas within which potentially cooperative pairs may get to know each other better— the golf courses, the civic clubs, the voluntary associations— any way that valid relationships may be developed. As successful managers (and con men) have long recognized, very high dividends may be gained by remembering to spend some effort and time at this phase—to delay plunging into riskier enterprises until more informal, less impersonal relationships have been established. Once the conversion is accomplished, the closer bonds will prove more profitable.

Finally, we might speculate on the meaning of the findings of this research for what, except for the family, is probably the largest arena of cooperation—the organized work engaged in by employees of corporate or bureaucratic organizations. The growth of such organizations has been traced to various of their characteristics, including rationity and the ability to accumulate capital. But consider also the effect of such organizations on interpersonal risk. Where people are paid fixed salaries to cooperate, at least one potentially exploitable resource is fixed. Thus one of the key properties of organizations promoting cooperation may simply be its means of handling the risk problem.

On the other hand, the oft-noted inefficiency of such impersonal organizations might also be a result of their inability to handle risk. Employees may exploit the company by gold-bricking. Or they may fail to cooperate with each other, especially if they are also competing for promotions, and good performance may be claimed unilaterally by one or more potential co-workers. To date, contingencies have not been developed at the organizational level which are sufficient in themselves to always, or even usually, achieve optimum coordination and efficiency. Thus large organizations are never single entities striving as one toward a specific end. They must grapple with the problems of cohesiveness and cooperation among individuals. Even for them, cooperation may still be *the* question.

AN EXPERIMENT COMPARING SOCIAL COORDINATION IN THE COHEN–LINDSLEY AND MODIFIED SETTINGS

This experiment was designed to answer the question as to whether subjects working on the original (Cohen–Lindsley) or modified task could achieve high rates of cooperation even when they had no way of observing their partner's response (via the response light on the subject's panel which flashed whenever the partner made a task response). As we noted in Chapter 2, nonsocial cooperation, i.e., cooperation without the use of the response light, might be achieved in the original setting either by using the time-out light as a signal to respond, or by responding individually at very high rates. Therefore, to determine if cooperation depended on the response lights and/or time-out lights, the consequences of their presence or absence were investigated.

METHOD

Six pairs of college students (four female and two male) were studied for four 2-hour sessions, two sessions on each task. Half of the pairs worked first on the original task; half on the modified task.

The apparatus used for the modified task was identical to that described in Chapter 2, except that the task selection switch was covered and therefore unavailable. For the Cohen–Lindsley task, the same apparatus was programmed as follows: A cooperative response, defined when subjects pulled their plungers within 0.5 seconds of one another, was reinforced by a counter advance. An "individual" response, defined when either of the subjects pulled his plunger twice in a row without either of the pulls being part of a team response, was followed by a 2.5-second time-out accompanied by a loud tone. Each cooperative response was followed by a 5-second time-out during which the panel light went out.

At the beginning of the first session with either of the tasks, subjects received a brief description of the reinforcement contingencies over an intercom and made several reinforced responses. No stimulus changes were made during the first 2-hour session using a given task.

During the second session, subjects worked under four different conditions defined by the presence and/or absence of the response and time-out lights. This sequence is shown in Table A-1. In the third and fourth sessions, subjects repeated this sequence but worked on the other task.

Table A-1[a]

Conditions Defining Task Comparison Experiment

Condition	Minutes
1. Time-out and response lights	20
2. Time-out lights only	20
3. Response lights only	20
4. No lights	20
5. Time-out and response lights	20

[a]The above order was used with four pairs. For the other two pairs the order was Condition 1, 4, 3, 2, 5. Before Conditions 2, 3, and 4 subjects were told which lights would be inoperative.

RESULTS AND DISCUSSION

Figure A-1 compares cooperative response rates under the five stimulus conditions for each task. As the figure shows, only with the modified task did cooperation depend solely on the presence of the response lights. On the Cohen–Lindsley task, cooperative response rates were moderate to high under all conditions. In the absence of response lights, subjects tended to pull simultaneously when the time-out lights went out. With the absence of both response and time-out lights, substantial coordination was obtained either by responding rhythmically throughout the time-out or by responding individually at a high rate.

On the modified task, the rates of cooperation were

near zero with the response lights off, and moderate to high in all conditions with the response lights present. Thus the achievement of high rates of cooperation in this setting clearly requires that the behavior be "social."

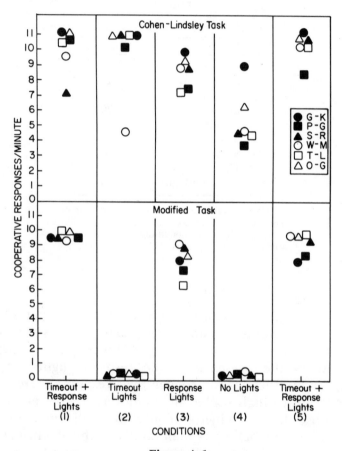

Figure A-1

The findings with the Cohen–Lindsley task indicate that the presence of either the response or timeout stimuli can result in a high rate of cooperation. However, they do not indicate which stimulus tends to be used when both are present. Additional data were obtained to explore this point. Previous research with the apparatus indicated that a reaction time of at least .2 second was required for a subject to respond if he were using the other's pull (response light) as a discriminative stimulus. Thus if the subject pulling second is responding to the behavior of the other, few of his pulls should fall within .2 seconds of his partner's. On the other hand, if both subjects are responding to the time-out stimulus, near-simultaneous responses are likely to occur, and a substantial proportion of the "second" responses should fall within this interval. Similarly, with the modified task, where the data indicate that the response light is required for a cooperative response, few of the second responses should fall within a .2-second interval following termination of the response light.

The results from the original task with both stimuli present indicated that response intervals of less than .2 seconds occurred in more than 80% of the cooperative responses for three of the six pairs, and in less than 20% of the responses for the remaining three. Under the modified task with both stimuli present, response intervals of less than .2 second occurred in no more than 2% of the cooperative responses for any pair. Thus we conclude that social coordination was necessary in the modified task, but that half the pairs were coordinating mainly on a non-social basis on the original Cohen–Lindsley version.

Adams, J. S. Inequity as social exchange. In L. Berkowitz (Ed.), *Advances in experimental social psychology.* Vol. II. New York: Academic Press, 1965. Pp. 267–99.

Aronson, E., & Carlsmith, J. M. Experimentation in social psychology. In L. Berkowitz (Ed.), *Advances in experimental social psychology.* Vol. 2. (2nd ed.) Reading, Massachusetts: Addison–Wesley, 1968. Pp. 1–79.

Azrin, N. H., & Holz, W. C. Punishment. In W. Honig (Ed.), *Operant behavior: Areas of research and application.* New York: Appleton, 1966. Pp. 380–447.

Azrin, N. H., & Lindsley, O. R. The reinforcement of cooperation between children. *Journal of Abnormal and Social Psychology,* 1956, **52,** 100–102.

195

Bixenstine, V. E., Levitt, C. A., & Wilson, N. V. Collaboration among six persons in a prisoner's dilemma game. *Journal of Conflict Resolution,* 1966, **10,** 488–96.

Blumstein, P. W., & Weinstein, E. A. Redress of distributive injustice. *The American Journal of Sociology,* 1969, **74,** 408–18.

Campbell, O. T., & Stanley, J. C. *Experimental and quasi-experimental designs for research.* Chicago: Rand McNally, 1963.

Cannavale, F. J., Scarr, H. A., & Pepitone, A. Deindividuation in a small group: Further evidence. *Journal of Personality and Social Psychology,* 1970, **16,** 141–7.

Charters, W. W., & Newcomb, T. M. Some attitudinal effects of experimentally increased salience of a membership group. In E. Macoby, T. Newcomb & E. Hartley (Eds.), *Readings in social psychology.* (3rd ed.) New York: Holt, 1958. Pp. 276–81.

Cohen, D. J. Justin and his peers: An experimental analysis of a child's social world. *Child Development,* 1962, **33,** 697–717.

Deutsch, M. A theory of cooperation and competition. *Human Relations,* 1949, **2,** 129–52.

Deutsch, M. An experimental study of the effects of cooperation and competition upon group process. *Human Relations,* 1949, **2,** 199–231.

Deutsch, M. Cooperation and trust: some theoretical notes. In M. R. Jones, (Ed.), *Nebraska symposium on motivation, 1962.* Lincoln, Nebraska: University of Nebraska Press, 1962. Pp. 275–318.

Deutsch, M., & Krauss, R. M. Studies of interpersonal bargaining. *Journal of Conflict Resolution,* March 1962, **6,** 52–76.

Druckman, D. The influence of the situation in interparty conflict. *Conflict Resolution.* 1971, **15,** 523–54.

Egerman, K. Effects of team arrangement on team performance: A learning theoretic analysis. *Journal of Personality and Social Psychology,* 1966, **3,** 541–50.

Ferster, C. B., & Skinner, B. F. *Schedules of reinforcement.* New York: Appleton, 1957.

Festinger, L., Pepitone, A., & Newcomb, T. Some consequences of deindividuation in a group. *Journal of Abnormal and Social Psychology,* 1952, **47,** 382–89.

Ghiselli, E. E., & Lodahl, T. M. Patterns of managerial traits and group effectiveness. *Journal of Abnormal and Social Psychology,* 1958, **57,** 61–6.

Hake, D., & Vukelich, R. A classification and review of cooperation procedures. *Journal of the Experimental Analsis of Behavior,* 1972, **18,** 333–43.

Homans, G. C. *Social behavior: Its elementary forms.* New York: Harcourt, Brace, & World, 1961.

Horowitz, I. L. *Professing sociology.* Chicago: Aldine, 1968.

Keller, F. S., & Schoenfeld, W. N. *Principles of psychology.* New York: Appleton, 1950.

Kelley, H. H. Experimental studies of threats in interpersonal negotiations. *Journal of Conflict Resolution,* 1965, **9,** 79–105.

Kelley, H., & Thibaut, J. Group problem solving. In G. Lindsey & E. Aronson (Eds.), *The handbook of social psychology.* Vol. IV. (2nd ed.) Reading, Massachusetts: Addison–Wesley, 1969. Pp. 1–101.

Kelman, H. Human use of human subjects: The problem of deception in social psychological experiments. *Psychological Bulletin,* 1967, **67,** 1–11.

Krauss, R., & Deutsch, M. Communication in interpersonal bargaining. *Journal of Personality and Social Psychology,* 1966, **4,** 572–77.

Leavitt, H. Some effects of certain communication patterns in group performance. In E. E. Maccoby, T. M. Newcomb, & E. L. Hartley (Eds.), *Readings in social psychology.* (3rd ed.) New York: Holt, 1958. Pp. 546–63.

Lerner, M. J. The justice motive: "Equity" and "parity" among children. *Journal of Personality and Social Psychology,* 1974, **29,** 439–50.

Leventhal, G. S., Allen, J., & Kemelgor, B. Reducing inequity by reallocating rewards. *Psychonomic Science,* 1969, **14,** 295–96.

Leventhal, G., & Anderson, D. Self-interest and the maintenance of equity. *Journal of Personality and Social Psychology,* 1970, **15,** 57–62.

Leventhal, G. S., & Bergman, J. T. Self-depriving behavior as a response to unprofitable inequity. *Journal of Experimental Social Psychology,* 1969, **5,** 153–71.

Leventhal, G. S., Weiss, T., & Long, G. Equity, reciprocity, and reallocating rewards in the dyad. *Journal of Personality and Social Psychology,* 1969, **13,** 300–305.

Lindsley, O. R. Experimental analysis of cooperation and competition. In T. Verhave (Ed.), *The experimental analysis of behavior.* New York: Appleton, 1966. Pp. 470–501.

Luce, R. D., & Raiffa, H. *Games and decisions.* New York: Wiley, 1957.

Lundberg, G., Schrag, C., & Larsen, O. *Sociology.* (3rd ed.) New York: Harper & Row, 1963.

Lutzker, D. R. Sex role, cooperation and competition in a two-person, non-zero-sum game. *Journal of Conflict Resolution,* 1961, **5,** 366–68.

Maller, J. B. *Cooperation and competition: An experimental study in motivation.* New York: Teachers College, Columbia University Contributions to Education, No. 384, 1929.

May, M. A., & Doob, L. W. *Competition and cooperation.* New York: Social Science Research Council, 1937.

Mayo, E. *The social problems of an industrial civilization.* Boston: Graduate School of Business Administration, Harvard University, 1945.

McNeel, S. P., McClintock, C. G., & Nuttin, J. M. Effects of sex role in a two-person mixed-motive game. *Journal of Personality and Social Psychology,* 1972, **24,** 372–80.

McNemar, Q. *Psychological statistics.* (4th ed.) New York: Wiley, 1969.

Mead, M. *Cooperation and competition among primitive people.* New York: McGraw–Hill, 1937.

Merton, R. *Social theory and social structure.* Glencoe, Illinois: The Free Press, 1957.

Mithaug, D. E. & Burgess, R. L. The effects of different reinforcement procedures in the establishment of group response. *Journal of Experimental Child Psychology,* 1968, **5,** 441–54.

Mumford, L. *Technics and civilization.* New York: Harcourt, Brace, 1934.

Nisbet, R. Cooperation. In *International encyclopedia of the social sciences.* Vol. 3. New York: Macmillan & The Free Press, 1968.

Ofshe, R. The effectiveness of pacifist strategies: A theoretical approach. *Journal of Conflict Resolution,* 1971, **15,** 261–69.

Oskamp, S. Effects of programmed strategies on cooperation in the prisoner's dilemma and other mixed-motive games. *Conflict Resolution,* 1971, **15,** 225–59.

Parsons, T. *The social system.* Glencoe, Illinois: Free Press, 1951.

Pillsuk, M., Winter, J. A., Chapman, R. & Hass, N. Honesty, deceit, and timing in the display of intentions. *Behavioral Science,* 1967, **12,** 205–12.

Pritchard, R. D. Equity theory: a review and critique, *Organizational Behavior and Human Performance,* 1969, **4,** 176–211.

Radlow, R. & Weidner, M. Unenforced commitments in "cooperative" and "non-cooperative" non-constant-sum games. *Journal of Conflict Resolution,* 1966, **10,** 497–505.

Rapoport, A. & Chammah, A. M. *Prisoner's dilemma.* Ann Arbor: University of Michigan Press, 1965.

Roby, T. B. *Small group performance.* Chicago: Rand McNally, 1968.

Rosenberg, S. & Hall, R. L. The effects of different social feedback conditions upon performance in dyadic teams. *Journal of Abnormal and Social Psychology,* 1958, **57,** 271–77.

Rosenthal, R. *Experimenter effects in behavioral research.* New York: Appleton, 1966.

Scodel, S., Minas, J. S., Ratoosh, P., & Lipetz, M. Some descriptive aspects of two-person non-zero-sum games. *Journal of Conflict Resolution,* 1959, **3,** 114–19.

Shure, G. H., Meeker, R. J., & Hansford, E. A. The effectiveness of pacifist strategies in bargaining games. *Journal of Conflict Resolution,* 1965, **9**, 106–17.

Sidman, M. *Tactics of scientific research.* New York: Basic Books, 1960.

Sidowski, J. B., Wyckoff, L. B., & Tabory, L. The influence of reinforcement and punishment in a minimal social situation. *Journal of Abnormal and Social Psychology,* 1956, **52**, 115–17.

Singer, J. E., Brush, C. A., and Lubin, S. C. Some aspects of deindividuation: Identification and conformity. *Journal of Experimental Social Psychology,* 1965, **1**, 356–78.

Smead, A. Cooperation and competition. In L. Wrightsman, *Social psychology in the seventies.* Belmont, California: Brooks/Cole, 1972, Pp. 131–55.

Smelser, W. T. Dominance as a factor in achievement and perception in cooperative problem solving interactions. *Journal of Abnormal and Social Psychology,* 1961, **62**, 535–42.

Swennson, R. G. Cooperation in the prisoner's dilemma game: I. the effects of asymmetric payoff information and explicit communication. *Behavioral Science,* 1967, **12**, 314–22.

Swingle, P. (Ed.), *The structure of conflict.* New York: Academic Press, 1970.

Swingle, P. G., & Santi, A. Communication in non-zero-sum games. *Journal of Personality and Social Psychology,* 1972, **23**, 54–63.

Vinacke, W. E. Variables in experimental games: toward a field theory. *Psychological Bulletin,* 1969, **71**, 293–318.

Voissem, N.H., & Sistrunk, F., Communication schedule and cooperative game behavior. *Journal of Personality and Social Psychology,* 1971, **19**, 160–67.

Volger, R. E. On the definition of cooperation. *Psychological Reports,* 1969, **25**, 281–82.

Walster, E., Berscheid, E. & Walster, W. G. New directions in equity research. *Journal of Personality and Social Psychology,* 1973, **25**, 151–76.

Webb, E. W., Campbell, D. J., Schwartz, R. D., & Sechrest, L. *Unobtrusive measures: Nonreactive research in the social sciences.* Chicago: Rand–McNally, 1966.

Wegner, N. & Zeaman, D. Team and individual performances on a motor learning task. *The Journal of General Psychology,* 1956, **55**, 127–42.

Weiner, H. Response cost and the aversive control of human operant behavior, *Journal of the Experimental Analysis of Behavior,* 1963, **6**, 415–21.

Weingarten, R. & Mechner, F. The contingency as an independent variable of social interaction. In T. Verhave (Ed.), *The experimental analysis of behavior.* New York: Appleton-Century-Crofts, 1966, 447–59.

Wiggins, J. A. Hypothesis validity and experimental laboratory methods. In H. M. Blalock, Jr., & A. B. Blalock (Eds.), *Methodology in social research.* New York: McGraw–Hill, 1968, Pp. 390–427.

Wichman, H. Effects of isolation and communication on cooperation in a two-person game. *Journal of Personality and Social Psychology,* 1970, **16,** 114–20.

Zajonc, R. *Social psychology: An experimental approach.* Belmont, California: Wadsworth, 1966.

Zimbardo, P. G. The human choice: Individuation, reason, and order versus deindividuation, impulse and chaos. In W. J. Arnold and D. Levine (Eds.), *Nebraska symposium on motivation, 1969.* Lincoln: University of Nebraska Press, 1970, 237–307.

AUTHOR INDEX

A

Adams, J. S., 13, 55
Allen, J., 44
Anderson, D., 44, 50
Aristotle, 2
Aronson, E., 184
Azrin, N. H., 20, 24

B

Bergman, J. T., 44

Bixenstine, V. E., 127
Blumstein, P. W., 44
Brush, C. A., 187
Burgess, R. L., 20

C

Campbell, O. T., 24, 50
Cannavale, F. J., 187
Carlsmith, J. M., 184
Chammah, A. M., 59, 105
Chapman, R., 127

SUBJECT INDEX

A

Aggression, 163, 167, 169
Agreements between subjects, 60,
    127, 130–133, 135–136, 140,
    141, 148
  broken, 127, 131–132
Alienation, 179
Anonymity, *see* Personalization
Avoidance, 122–123, 136–137
  anticipatory, 119

Avoidance *(continued)*
  free-operant, 119–127
  signaled, 114–118, 126

B

Baseline conditions, defined, 32,
    38
Boredom in experiments, 24–25
  and alternative tasks, 21

205